Enlargement of the EU and The Treaty of Nice

FINANCIAL TIMES

Prentice Hall

In an increasingly competitive world, we believe it's
quality of thinking that will give you the edge – an idea
that opens new doors, a technique that solves a problem, or
an insight that simply makes sense of it all. The more you
know, the smarter and faster you can go.

That's why we work with the best minds in business
and finance to bring cutting-edge thinking and best
learning practice to a global market.

Under a range of leading imprints, including
Financial Times Prentice Hall, we create world-class
print publications and electronic products bringing our
readers knowledge, skills and understanding which can
be applied whether studying or at work.

To find out more about our business publications, or tell
us about the books you'd like to find, you can visit us at
www.business-minds.com

For other Pearson Education publications, visit
www.pearsoned-ema.com

Pearson
Education

Enlargement of the EU and The Treaty of Nice

H M SCOBIE

An imprint of Pearson Education

London ■ New York ■ Toronto ■ Sydney ■ Tokyo ■ Singapore ■ Hong Kong ■ Cape Town
New Delhi ■ Madrid ■ Paris ■ Amsterdam ■ Munich ■ Milan ■ Stockholm

PEARSON EDUCATION LIMITED

Head Office:
Edinburgh Gate
Harlow CM20 2JE
Tel: +44 (0)1279 623623
Fax: +44 (0)1279 431059

London Office:
128 Long Acre
London WC2E 9AN
Tel: +44 (0)20 7447 2000
Fax: +44 (0)20 7240 5771
Website: www.briefingzone.com

First published in Great Britain in 2002

© H.M. Scobie 2002

The right of H.M. Scobie to be identified as Author
of this Work has been asserted by her in accordance
with the Copyright, Designs and Patents Act 1988.

ISBN 0 273 65925 1

British Library Cataloguing in Publication Data
A CIP catalogue record for this book can be obtained from the British Library.

10 9 8 7 6 5 4 3 2 1

Typeset by Monolith – www.monolith.uk.com
Printed and bound in Great Britain by Ashford Colour Press Ltd, Gosport, Hants.

The Publishers' policy is to use paper manufactured from sustainable forests.

About the author

Professor Scobie MSc(London), PhD(Cantab) graduated from the London School of Economics and received a PhD from Cambridge University. She became Director of the European Economics & Financial Centre in 1989 and Professor of Economics at the University of London in 1993 and has also been serving as a Registered Representative of the London Stock Exchange.

Professor Scobie has published numerous books in the field of economics and finance. Among the books are *Treasury and Debt Management*, *European Monetary Union: the Way Forward*, *The European Single Market*, *Economic Policy Coordination in an Integrating Europe*, *The Euro Bond Market*, *Structural Changes in European Pension Funds*, *Reserve Management* and *Impact of the Euro for the European Fixed Income Market*.

She has been advisor to the European Commission and many governments on a variety of economics and financial projects. She has advised the US Government on the relationship of taxation and attraction of foreign investment, the UK Parliament on the implication of European Monetary Union for Britain, etc.

Professor Scobie has completed two major projects commissioned by the International Securities Markets Association (ISMA) working with some 900 banks across Europe (in 1997) on the preparations for the transition to the euro; and (in 1999/2000) on the implication of the euro for the fixed income market.

She has been a member of the Market Practices Committee of the International Swaps and Derivatives Association (ISDA).

Professor Scobie has also published over 100 articles, the most important of which is the work on 'A Global Single Currency: the Inevitable Direction'.

Professor Scobie may be contacted at:

European Economic & Financial Centre
20 Guildford Street
London WC1N 1DZ

Tel: +44(0) 0207 229 0402
Fax: +44(0) 0207 221 5118
Email: eefc@eefc.com

Contents

Tables

Acknowledgements

Many members of the European Economics and Financial Centre assisted with the preparation of this book. I am indebted to them for their assistance and support with the research work towards the production of this volume. In particular I wish to thank the following: B. Allan, A. Cormack, J. Frendak, S. Klimenko, A. Gustapane, S. Michaux, S. Adamo, N. Baker, V. Bewaji and D. Robinson. I would also like to thank Mr Darren Davy and Dr John Hall for their support and encouragement. The assistance of Nexus Capital – Affiliate of Soros Fund Management LLC towards this study is acknowledged. Finally special thanks go to George Soros who has been the inspiration behind this book.

Executive summary

The objectives of this book are multifold. First, it is designed to explain the requirements for entry into the European Union (EU) by an applicant country. For an outsider, deciphering the volume of material on EU entry can be quite arduous. This book is designed to act as a basic guide, outlining in a concise manner the procedure for joining the EU.

Second, it offers a comprehensive analysis of the countries in line for accession to the EU. Third, the book provides an independent assessment of the prospects for each of the candidate countries becoming unified with the EU. A comprehensive survey of the 13 applicant countries has been carried out for this purpose. The survey contains an in-depth appraisal of the developments of these markets and provides a checklist of the key requirements for EU entry, together with projections for their accession. This survey also includes the views of existing member states who are the ultimate decision makers for admission of the EU hopefuls.

The analyses are put forward with a view to providing unbiased and independent information on the process of decision-making *vis-à-vis* the future EU membership prospects of these states. It brings to the fore the views of different sides, i.e. the applicant countries as well as the EU institutions making the final judgements for the enlargement of the EU. The book also gives a full account of all the reforms of the EU institutions in laying the foundation for the accession of these countries.

The book comprises three parts:

- Part one consisting of Chapters 1 and 2 – gives an overview of the entry requirements in the form of methodology and practice in that order. Chapter 1 enumerates the entry requirements and the procedures followed. Chapter 2 demonstrates the methodology in practice and provides projections for the timing of accession for the group of 13 applicant countries.

- Part two covering Chapters 3–15 – contains an analysis and a checklist of the state of preparedness of each candidate country and its potential accession date.

- Part three containing Chapter 16 – examines the structural reforms designed to facilitate the process of enlargement that have been introduced at the Nice Summit and may be further needed for EU institutions.

The entire group of existing applicant countries are covered in this book. They are:

- Poland
- Czech Republic
- Hungary
- Estonia

- Slovenia
- Cyprus
- Latvia
- Slovakia
- Malta
- Lithuania
- Bulgaria
- Romania
- Turkey.

The book, being based on independent research, is designed to serve as a reference to the enlargement procedure – offering a 'countdown' to accession. A brief explanation of each part is given below.

Part one

In this part Chapter 1 examines the procedure from the time a country submits an application to the time when it finally becomes united with the EU. It brings to light the roles of decision makers both within the EU institutions and across the different EU member states.

Chapter 2 analyses the likely dates for the applicant countries to join the EU. The analysis of timing of entry also takes into account the dates when reforms proposed for the European Council, the European Commission and the European Parliament come into effect.

Part two

Part two consists of 13 chapters (Chapters 3–15) – one devoted to each applicant country. Each chapter critically examines the position and progress of the accession country concerned. It examines whether the aspiring country meets the criteria for entry (based on the Copenhagen Criteria of 1993). These chapters also provide analyses of timing of their accession and appraise the country's prospects for joining.

The country chapters review each state's efforts in reforming its economy since the fall of the Iron Curtain. They spell out how these economies differ from those of the existing members of the EU – highlighting their weaknesses and pointing out the extent of further work required on their part. Part two also illuminates some of the developments that have gone unnoticed by the decision makers in Western economies.

Among the issues that are addressed for each country are:

- essential macroeconomic characteristics of the applicant country;
- the make-up and constraints of the infrastructure of the country;

■ the role of the government within each of the candidate countries.

The analysis identifies the pattern and type of reform imposed by the Commission as requirements for each country's entry. These chapters also cover the speed of fulfilment of the criteria for all the accession countries. The variables are assessed both from the country's viewpoint and from the viewpoint of the EU decision makers.

Part three

The reform of EU institutions agreed at the Nice Summit was intended to provide the necessary steps for the smooth functioning of these organizations in order to cater for an EU with up to 28–30 members. Part three embracing Chapter 16 presents the structural changes that are envisaged for the European institutions, which in turn could accommodate EU enlargement.

In laying the foundation for a manageable enlargement of the EU, a good grasp of two critical factors is imperative:

■ a thorough understanding of the manner in which EU institutions operate presently;

■ a thorough understanding of the manner in which EU institutions will be operating in future to service a Union with increased membership.

Throughout this book, primary information on all parts of the study is provided and the thinking of all the decision makers involved is presented.

Part one

1

Transformation of the EU and procedures for EU entry

3

INTRODUCTION

This book presents an overview of the enlargement of the European Union (EU). It explains the steps involved for an applicant country to accede to the EU. In this respect it can serve as a 'countdown' for an accession country.

The book also examines the likely timeframe within which different applicant countries could effectively join the EU. For such an assessment it is necessary to ascertain how, in practice, a new member is admitted and to explain the procedure involved. For any aspiring country to be admitted to the EU the following decisions are required:

■ the decision of the country to apply and subsequently be willing to make all the necessary changes to comply with the rules and regulations of the EU;

■ the decision of the European Commission to 'recommend' that the candidate has satisfied all the EU entry requirements and that the applicant country be admitted to the Union;

■ the approval of each of the existing member countries of the EU (collectively forming the European Council), whose decisions will in turn be based on:

 – each country's own internal assessment

 – reports and recommendations of the European Commission.

Thus, for the purpose of this study, it was essential to obtain independently of each other the views of three separate categories involved in the EU enlargement:

■ the opinion and assessment of the countries in line for accession to the EU;

■ the opinion and assessment of the European Commission;

■ the opinion and assessment of the existing EU member states.

These are covered both in this chapter and in subsequent chapters covering each applicant country (Chapters 3–15).

ACCESSION BACKGROUND OF THE EXISTING EU MEMBERS

To throw light upon the future of the enlargement of the EU, it is useful to provide an overview of the evolution of the EU as it stands in 2001 (with 15 member states).

The origins of the EU date back to 1952 when the original six European states shown in Table 1.1 signed the Coal and Steel Agreement. However, the formalization of the EU only commenced in 1957 with the signing of the Treaty of Rome. This grouping was then named the European Economic Community (EEC).

Table 1.1 Evolution of the EU

Date of joining the EU	Countries that joined	Cumulative total number of member states	Additional comments
1952	Coal and Steel Community	6	Origin of the EU when the six European states set out to form a common market in the coal and steel industries
1957	Belgium France Germany Italy Luxembourg Netherlands	6	Foundation of the EU, known at that time as the EEC or 'Common Market'
1973	Denmark Ireland UK	9	
1981	Greece	10	
1986	Portugal Spain	12	
1995	Austria Finland Sweden	15	

The six founder member states of the EEC were:

1 Belgium

2 France

3 Germany

4 Italy

5 Luxembourg

6 Netherlands.

Subsequently, there has been a rather sporadic flow of new members, notably in 1973 when three countries joined:

7 Denmark

8 Ireland

9 UK.

Their membership was a comparatively straightforward process since these states were economically, politically and socially developed and compatible with the then six existing members. Following in their path were, in 1981:

10 Greece

and two more in 1986:

11 Portugal

12 Spain.

Finally, in 1995, the following three rather wealthier states joined:

13 Austria

14 Finland

15 Sweden.

These countries constitute the 15-member EU that is active in 2002. The shape of the EU is likely to remain the same at least until 2004 – based on the indicators and official statements made up to the end of 2002. This issue will be elaborated on in the course of the study.

Norway applied to join the EU (at the time known as the 'Common Market') in March 1972 and subsequently withdrew its application in October 1972, following a referendum in which the majority of the voters were against signing. There was a second referendum in 1995, which was again unfavourable.

PROCESS OF EU ACCESSION FOR A COUNTRY

In the Introduction on page 5 an overview of all the final decisions required in the accession of a country to the EU was given. However, in practice before each decision is reached there are many stages involved in the process of accession. This can make the procedure quite drawn out. An overview of these stages is provided in the studies of each applicant state in Chapters 3–15. For each country in line for accession, there is a table that outlines the country's evolving relationship with the EU. However, broadly speaking the procedure for the membership of the EU tends to follow the pattern shown below:

1 Usually, prior to submitting an application for membership, an agreement is signed with the EU, which is named the 'Europe Agreement'. This agreement is also known as the 'Association Agreement'. It is an agreement between member countries and candidates on issues such as trade, political dialogue, the environment, transport, etc. At times there can be several years between the signing of the Europe Agreement and formal application for EU membership.

2 Following a formal application from a country for membership of the EU, the European Council tends to respond on average after a year. If it is in principle favourable towards examination of the applicant's membership, the Council allows for 'Consultation of the European Commission' to commence.

3 The European Commission examines the compatibility of the country with the laws and requirements of the EU and on this basis presents an Opinion to the European Council recommending whether or not the country should become an 'official applicant' and that the pre-accession preparations should commence.

4 Subsequently the Commission reviews the country's position and recommends whether or not the so-called 'accession negotiations' should commence. This is when the applicant becomes a serious candidate. In effect the Commission recommends to the member states (which represent the EU in accession talks) to open formally the accession negotiations with the applicant country.

5 Following either of the above two stages, the European Council comprising the member states examines the views of the Commission, and on the basis of the 'Opinion' expressed in the report and its own views, the Council endorses the recommendation of the Commission and in the case mentioned above endorses the opening of the so-called 'accession negotiations'. Subsequently the country wishing to join provides an overview of where it stands on all the *acquis communautaire* chapters (the body of common rights and obligations that bind all the member states together within the EU) and then initiates discussions with the member states.

6 The country holding the six-month rotating presidency of the Council of Ministers tables the negotiating aims of the EU. Moreover, the country holding the presidency chairs all the sessions covering the negotiations at the level of ministers or their deputies. For example, the Council approves how many and which of the 31 chapters of the *acquis communautaire* are to be opened and provisionally closed.

In 1997, for instance, the European Commission presented an Opinion on Poland's and Estonia's applications for EU membership. Based on the recommendations of the Commission, the European Council concluded that accession negotiations should open with these countries. The actual accession negotiations commenced in March 1998.

On the other hand, the Commission 1989 Opinion on Turkey's application for EU membership concluded that: 'Turkey's economic and political situation ... does not convince the Commission that the adjustment problems which would confront Turkey if it were to accede to the Community could be overcome in the medium term'. In 1999, based on the recommendations of the Commission, the European Council in Helsinki chose to admit Turkey as an official EU applicant. Nevertheless, it still did not find the country sufficiently prepared for the opening of accession negotiations. However, from the year 2000 Turkey has been undergoing pre-accession preparation.

The reports produced by the European Commission prior to 1998 were entitled 'Commission Opinion'. From 1998 they were renamed as the 'Commission Regular Report' or the 'Commission Progress Report'.

7   In the course of the accession negotiations, each applicant country has to satisfy the three main components of entry requirements, namely the political criteria, the economic criteria and 31 chapters of the *acquis communautaire* (explained in detail below).

The fulfilment of these requirements, in particular the closing of the different chapters of the *acquis*, act as a countdown towards the final entry date.

8   Once all the requirements have been satisfied, the Commission recommends admission to the EU and a Draft Accession Treaty is prepared.

9   The European Council has to approve and sign the Draft Treaty. This Draft Treaty is also passed on to the European Parliament for agreement.

10 Each of the existing member states and the applicant country must then get the approval of their own parliaments for the accession of the candidate country to the EU.[1] This stage is expected to last 18 months for this round of applicant countries.

For some countries the fulfilment of the *acquis* chapters takes several years. Yet for a country such as Norway, the entire list of *acquis* chapters were satisfactorily negotiated and concluded over a period of some nine months. However, in the end Norway did not join because the referendum it had held shortly before the accession did not allow it to join the EU either in 1972 or in 1995.

The country wishing to join provides an overview of where it stands *vis-à-vis* all the *acquis* chapters and then initiates discussions with the member states.

11 After the approval of all the member states, the Draft Treaty becomes the Treaty and takes effect. At that point the applicant country becomes a member state on the date that has been determined for accession. Technically a country can join at any time in a given year. However, in practice the preferred date seems to be the beginning of a calendar year, since this is also the beginning of the fiscal year that encompasses the financial arrangements for all the member states, including the new member.

REQUIREMENTS OF ENTRY INTO THE EU

The requirements of entry into the EU fall under three categories:

■ political criteria;

■ economic criteria;

■ 'ability to assume obligations of membership' including adherence to the rules and regulations[2] of the EU, comprising 31 chapters of the *acquis communautaire*.

The political criteria and economic criteria were set out at the June 1993 Copenhagen European Council during the Danish presidency. These requirements for entry are known as the Copenhagen Criteria. Accordingly, accession to the EU occurs as soon as an applicant is able to meet the above conditions.[3]

Political criteria[4]

As the Copenhagen European Council postulated, for each candidate country to join the EU it has to satisfy certain political conditions. More specifically, it demands that certain institutions of the country have to be stable. Such institutions are those that ensure:

1 democracy
2 the rule of law
3 human rights
4 respect and protection of minorities.

These conditions can become clearer if they are seen in the context of candidate countries. Slovakia, for instance, needed to develop its parliamentary democracy in order to satisfy the political criteria. Romania was required to incorporate homosexual rights into its national law (among other reforms), while in Estonia the minority Russian speakers (those whose mother tongue is Russian) were required to be granted equal rights. An example of a country that has so far not been able to meet any conditions of the political criteria is Turkey. Fulfilment of all the above conditions has remained a concern for the EU.

However, concluding whether or not a country has fully met the political criteria is rather a grey area. The interpretation of the Commission statements on political criteria is discussed further in Chapter 2.

Economic criteria

Membership to the EU requires:

- the existence of a functioning market economy;
- the capacity to cope with the competitive pressure and market forces within the Union.

For a country to demonstrate that it has an operational 'market economy' it has to fulfil several requirements:

1 Equilibrium between demand and supply:
   - free interplay of market forces;
   - liberalization of prices.

2   Absence of barriers to market entry and exit.

3   Soundness of the legal system, including:

   ■ regulation of property rights;

   ■ enforceability of laws and contracts.

4   Achievement of macroeconomic stability, including:

   ■ price stability;

   ■ sustained public finances;

   ■ external accounts.

5   A broad consensus on economic policy.

6   A sufficiently developed financial sector, with the ability to channel savings towards investment.

The requirement of having 'the capacity to cope with competitive pressure and market forces within the Union' is quite demanding for some of the poorer central and Eastern European countries. Indeed there exists a vast divergence between the income of the existing EU members and some of the countries of Eastern Europe.

   At the European Parliament on 16 July 1997 when Agenda 2000 was put forward, it was stated that none of the applicant countries were thought to have a functioning market economy able to compete in the EU. However, several states were thought to be close. These included Hungary, Poland, the Czech Republic and Slovenia. Slovakia was judged to be able to compete, but not to have a functioning market economy.

   As far as the fulfilment of the economic criteria is concerned, substantial progress was made by some of the applicant countries in the late 1990s.

Ability to assume obligations of membership

For each applicant country to join the EU, it has to satisfy all chapters of what is named the *acquis communautaire*. The exact definition of the *acquis* is:[5]

The Community acquis *or Community patrimony is the body of common rights and obligations which bind all the Member States together within the European Union.*

   It is constantly evolving and comprises:

■ *the content, principles and political objectives of the treaties*

■ *the legislation adopted in application of the treaties and the case law of the Court of Justice*

■ *the declarations and resolutions adopted by the Union*

■ *measures relating to justice and home affairs*

■ *international agreements concluded by the Community and those concluded by the Member States between themselves in the field of the Union's activities.*

Applicant countries have to accept the Community acquis *before they can join the European Union. Exemptions and derogations from the acquis are granted in only exceptional circumstances and are limited in scope.*

The *acquis communautaire* comprises 31 chapters, the headings of which are listed below:

1 Free movement of goods

2 Freedom of movement for persons

3 Freedom to provide services

4 Free movement of capital

5 Company law

6 Competition policy

7 Agriculture

8 Fisheries

9 Transport policy

10 Taxation

11 Economic and monetary union

12 Statistics

13 Social policy and employment

14 Energy

15 Industrial policy

16 Small and medium-sized undertakings

17 Science and research

18 Education and training

19 Telecommunications and information technologies

20 Culture and audio-visual policy

21 Regional policy and co-ordination of structural instruments

22 Environment

23 Consumers and health protection

24 Co-operation in the fields of justice and home affairs

25 Customs union

26 External relations

27 Common foreign and security policy

28 Financial control

29 Financial and budgetary provisions

30 Institutions

31 Other

These 31 chapters are also used for the purpose of the screening exercise with respect to start of the accession negotiations outlined above.

Although in reality there are 31 chapters of the *acquis*, in practice the European Commission lists 29 chapters in its publications providing a progress report on the countries. The last two chapters – 'institutions' and 'others' – are left to the very end of the negotiations. For this reason, all the references are to the 29 chapters of the *acquis*.

Meeting the requirements of the political and economic criteria are quite separate from complying with all the chapters of the *acquis*. The *acquis* is the third requirement, which falls under ability to assume obligations of membership. This is examined for each country in the forthcoming chapters.

METHOD OF ASSESSMENT OF CANDIDATE COUNTRIES

The eligibility of any country wishing to join the EU has to be examined, based on the Copenhagen Criteria. Accordingly all the required information has to be obtained. For this purpose, all the facts and the relevant data are gathered through a variety of methods, namely through:

■ questionnaires sent to each country;

■ oral or written questions;

■ questioning of government representatives in committee meetings.

The scrutiny of the parliament of candidate countries usually takes place in the committees responsible for EU affairs.[6]

To assess the eligibility of any aspiring member, the European Commission carries out all the ground work in line with the conditions set out in the Copenhagen Criteria. Account is also taken of:

■ assessments made by each member state;

■ European Parliament Reports and Resolution;

■ the work of other international organizations, international financial institutions (IFIs), and non-governmental organizations (NGOs).

With respect to the political criteria, for instance, the Commission assesses whether candidate countries are satisfying the requirements by exploring beyond the formal descriptions into the practice of democracy itself. The Commission assesses, for example, whether rights and freedoms are practised in daily life by examining political parties, the media and the non-government organizations (NGOs).

To assess the fulfilment of the economic criteria, the Commission considers, among other tasks, whether the building blocks for a market economy are in place within the candidate country. That is, the Commission examines whether the liberalization of trade and prices and the free interplay of market forces have taken place. It examines whether or not the barriers to market entry and exit (for new firms and businesses) exist for all firms. The Commission also evaluates whether a legal system exists that includes the regulation of property rights and ensures laws and contracts are enforced.

Reports are continually made on the progress of the applicant countries, with a contribution from a large team from the European Commission across different directorate-generals. These used to be entitled the 'Commission Opinion' up to 1997. From 1998 they were renamed the Commission Regular Report of a particular year. For each applicant country there is a responsible official leading a team at the European Commission dealing with all aspects of entry preparations for the country concerned. Each country official also has responsibility for three sectors dealing with all the applicant countries. In this way a matrix of responsibilities and expertise is put in place that deals with the entry requirements of candidates. These reports act as the basis for the European Council to take important decisions on the conduct of the negotiations.

MEETING EU STANDARDS

The Copenhagen Criteria, unlike the Maastricht Criteria, are not stipulated in a quantifiable form. That is, none of the three principle requirements for EU entry set out in the Copenhagen Criteria are expressed in a measurable form. For example, in the Maastricht Criteria as one of the conditions for entry into the European Monetary Union, the ratio of national debt to GDP of the country has to be less than 60 per cent of the country's Gross Domestic Product or this ratio has to be falling over time. On the contrary, the conditions formulated for assessing the eligibility of a country for membership are purely qualitative. The only area where there is an appearance of a quantifiable measure is in the third requirement – 'meeting the obligations of membership'. However, one should not interpret the number of the *acquis* chapters closed as a barometer of how prepared a country is or how close to accession a country might be. To use mathematical metaphor, while it is 'necessary' to pass all the *acquis* chapters, it is not 'sufficient', for there are some *acquis* chapters that are very important and some that are less important and much easier to satisfy.

TRANSITION PERIOD

In the terminology of the European Commission and other related institutions dealing with the issues of EU enlargement, a transition period is a period of grace given for 'adjustment'. It can be requested by an applicant country or an existing EU member country (or alternatively even a group of countries). It can be of different time lengths depending on the reason for which the 'transition period' is requested by (or granted to) the applicant for adjusting their capabilities, capacities or rules in relation to the subject of the transition. Examples are given below.

Transition period from the viewpoint of the EU

An example of a transition period desirable on the part of EU member states is that of 'mobility of labour' – reflecting a fear of large migration from Eastern Europe to the West. Chapter 2 of the *acquis communautaire* focuses on 'freedom of movement for persons'. This rule permits the citizens of any member state to have total freedom as to where they choose to work and there is no restriction on their participation within the labour market of any other member state. However, freedom of movement of labour is one of the areas in which the bordering countries to Eastern Europe, such as Austria and Germany, have expressed concern and have requested the so-called 'transition period' in permitting the workers of the candidate countries free access to the EU's job market. Originally Germany and Austria seemed to favour a transition period of up to ten years with respect to the freedom of movement of labour. However, in December 2000 a speech made by Chancellor Schröder in a border town (near Germany's border with Eastern Europe) hinted at a transition period of at least seven years with respect to the free movement of labour.

Transition period from the viewpoint of the applicant countries

Freedom of movement of labour is both a sensitive and rather controversial issue. The accession countries are not willing to accept the transition period proposed and wish to have the full freedom of labour movement from the outset once they join the EU.

Some of the accession countries are also requesting a transition period with respect to land ownership in their countries by other EU member states. This may be an issue upon which they may have to compromise, with respect to restrictions imposed upon them on the freedom of labour movement.

Notes

1   In some cases there may have to be a referendum within the existing member states to approve the entry of a new member.

2 In principle, each state must be adequately equipped and should have 'created the conditions for its integration through the adjustment of its administrative structures, so that European Community legislation transposed into national legislation is implemented effectively through appropriate administrative and judicial structures'.

3 European Commission (1997) Agenda 2000, (1), Communication of the Commission Strasbourg, 15 July, DOC 97/6.

4 Reference to political criteria can be seen in any Commission Regular Report on any of the 13 applicant countries. See, for example, European Commission (2000), *Regular Report on Poland's Progress Towards Accession*, November.

5 Description given by the European Commission.

6 See *European Parliament White Paper 1999b*.

2

Applicant countries and timing of accession

Chapters 1 and 2 are complementary to each other. Whereas in Chapter 1 the procedures for an EU applicant country are discussed, this chapter focuses on the actual applicant countries (13 in total) in line for accession outstanding in 2001.

APPLICANT COUNTRIES FOR EU ACCESSION

The countries that form the 13 applicant countries to the EU are:

 1 Poland
 2 Czech Republic
 3 Hungary
 4 Estonia
 5 Slovenia
 6 Malta
 7 Cyprus
 8 Latvia
 9 Lithuania
10 Slovakia
11 Bulgaria
12 Romania
13 Turkey

Of these, the following ten candidates are from Central and Eastern Europe:

 1 Poland
 2 Czech Republic
 3 Hungary
 4 Estonia
 5 Slovenia
 6 Latvia
 7 Lithuania
 8 Slovakia
 9 Bulgaria
10 Romania

The remaining three are from Southern Europe:

1 Malta
2 Cyprus
3 Turkey

OFFICIAL OPENING OF NEGOTIATIONS

The terminology used for official negotiations within the EU institutions is 'accession negotiations'. The process of EU accession is detailed for each aspiring country in a table in the relevant chapter for the country concerned (Chapters 3–15).

In December 1997, when the European Council met in Luxembourg, it decided to initiate a comprehensive enlargement process with the applicant countries of Central and Eastern Europe, as well as (at that time) with Cyprus. This followed the publication of the European Commission's Opinions on the progress of the candidate countries in 1997, after which the Commission began to submit regular reports to the Council on further progress achieved by each country. These reports serve as a basis for the Council to take decisions on the conduct of negotiations or their extension to other candidates on the basis of the accession criteria.

The EU divided the existing official applicants into two groups, as far as the date for the official opening of the 'accession negotiations' is concerned. The more advanced group consists of:

- Poland
- Czech Republic
- Hungary
- Estonia
- Slovenia
- Cyprus.

These countries began their accession negotiations in March 1998 following the go-ahead by the Luxembourg European Council meeting in December 1997.

The following countries started their accession negotiations in 2000:

- Latvia
- Lithuania
- Bulgaria
- Romania
- Slovakia
- Malta.

This does not mean, however, those countries that started negotiations earlier would necessarily be the first countries to join.

Turkey, however, was recognized as an official EU applicant in December 1999 at the Helsinki European Council and was given the go-ahead to commence pre-accession preparations.

PROGRESS AND STATE OF NEGOTIATIONS

The fulfilment of economic and political criteria is discussed for each applicant country in Chapters 3–15. This section analyses the state of preparedness for each applicant country by examining exactly how many chapters of the *acquis communautaire* have been 'provisionally closed' by each applicant country (*see* Table 2.1). The wording 'provisionally closed' is used by the European Commission because chapters could be re-opened again at any time during the accession negotiations. The table shows:

- chapters opened and still under negotiation (shown by the symbol O);
- chapters provisionally closed (shown by the symbol ✓);
- chapters for which the Commission has proposed provisional closure (shown by the symbol [✓]);
- chapters not yet opened to negotiation (shown by the symbol ~).

It would have been highly desirable to be able to work out an average length of time per *acquis* chapter – ascertaining how long it takes for an applicant country to satisfy and close an *acquis* chapter. This study showed a cross comparison for the length of time taken by each candidate to satisfy a chapter of the *acquis* could be rather misleading, for it is entirely dependent on the state of that chapter within the applicant country concerned. It is clear that some countries satisfy certain chapters faster than the others. That, in turn, is dependent upon where the country stood at the start of the negotiation and/or how fast the country is prepared to introduce the required changes.

Interpretation of the Copenhagen Criteria

In Chapter 1 it was explained that determining whether a country has fully met the political criteria is rather a grey area. The interpretation of the Commission's statements *vis-a-vis* the political criteria is further discussed in this chapter.

To an outsider, the interpretation of the wording of the Commission on the political criteria is confusing and at times rather difficult to grasp. For the Commission may imply that the political criteria have been fulfilled, even though it lists many problems that remain. In addition, the wording and the tone of the Commission analysis of the 'political criteria' have changed from previous years. The Commission Regular Reports stated in 1998 that the country in question '*fulfils* the political criteria'. However, in its 2000 Regular Reports the Commission used the wording 'continues to fulfil', which is not as strong or clear-cut. Indeed the expression 'continues to fulfill' has a tone of weakness embedded in it for there are also a number of outstanding problems are listed for each country for which more work is requested by the Commission. To anyone reading the Report for the first time, it implies that 'as yet' the country has not satisfied the political criteria – but that the country is trying and will one day meet the requirement.

Table 2.1a State of accession negotiations with respect to chapters of the *acquis communautaire* (as of start of 2001)

Acquis chapters provisionally closed	Cyprus	Estonia	Czech Rep.
1 Free movement of goods	✓	✓	✓
2 Freedom of movement for persons	O	O	O
3 Freedom to provide services	O	O	O
4 Free movement of capital	O	✓	O
5 Company law	✓	✓	O
6 Competition policy	O	O	O
7 Agriculture	O	O	O
8 Fisheries	✓	✓	✓
9 Transport policy	[✓]	O	O
10 Taxation	O	O	O
11 Economic and monetary union	✓	✓	✓
12 Statistics	✓	✓	✓
13 Social policy and employment	✓	✓	O
14 Energy	O	O	O
15 Industrial policy	✓	✓	✓
16 Small and medium-sized undertakings	✓	✓	✓
17 Science and research	✓	✓	✓
18 Education and training	✓	✓	✓
19 Telecommunications and information technologies	✓	✓	✓
20 Culture and audio-visual policy	✓	✓	O
21 Regional policy and co-ordination of structural instruments	O	O	O
22 Environment	O	O	O
23 Consumers and health protection	✓	✓	✓
24 Co-operation in the fields of justice and home affairs	O	O	O
25 Customs union	✓	O	✓
26 External relations	✓	✓	✓
27 Common foreign and security policy	✓	✓	✓
28 Financial control	✓	O	O
29 Financial and budgetary provisions	O	O	O
30 Institutions			
Total chapters opened	29	29	29
Total chapters provisionally closed	17	16	13

O = chapter opened, under negotiation; ✓ = chapter provisionally closed; [✓] = chapter for which the Commission has proposed provisional closure.

Source: European Commission (2000) Directorate-General Enlargement.

Table 2.1b State of accession negotiations with respect to chapters of the *acquis communautaire* (as of start of 2001)

Acquis chapters provisionally closed	Hungary	Slovenia	Poland
1 Free movement of goods	O	O	[✓]
2 Freedom of movement for persons	O	O	O
3 Freedom to provide services	O	✓	✓
4 Free movement of capital	O	O	O
5 Company law	O	✓	O
6 Competition policy	O	O	O
7 Agriculture	O	O	O
8 Fisheries	✓	✓	O
9 Transport policy	O	O	O
10 Taxation	O	O	O
11 Economic and monetary union	✓	✓	✓
12 Statistics	✓	✓	✓
13 Social policy and employment	✓	✓	O
14 Energy	✓	[✓]	O
15 Industrial policy	✓	✓	✓
16 Small and medium-sized undertakings	✓	✓	✓
17 Science and research	✓	✓	✓
18 Education and training	✓	✓	✓
19 Telecommunications and information technologies	✓	✓	✓
20 Culture and audio-visual policy	O	O	✓
21 Regional policy and co-ordination of structural instruments	O	O	O
22 Environment	O	O	O
23 Consumers and health protection	✓	✓	✓
24 Co-operation in the fields of justice and home affairs	O	O	O
25 Customs union	O	O	O
26 External relations	✓	O	✓
27 Common foreign and security policy	✓	✓	✓
28 Financial control	✓	✓	✓
29 Financial and budgetary provisions	O	O	O
30 Institutions			
Total chapters opened	29	29	29
Total chapters provisionally closed	14	14	13

O = chapter opened, under negotiation; ✓ = chapter provisionally closed; [✓] = chapter for which the Commission has proposed provisional closure.

Source: European Commission (2000) Directorate-General Enlargement.

Table 2.1c State of accession negotiations with respect to chapters of the *acquis communautaire* (as of start of 2001)

Acquis chapters provisionally closed	Malta	Latvia	Lithuania
1 Free movement of goods	~	~	~
2 Freedom of movement for persons	~	~	~
3 Freedom to provide services	~	O	O
4 Free movement of capital	O	O	O
5 Company law	✓	O	O
6 Competition policy	O	O	O
7 Agriculture	~	~	~
8 Fisheries	O	O	~
9 Transport policy	O	O	O
10 Taxation	~	~	~
11 Economic and monetary union	✓	✓	~
12 Statistics	✓	✓	✓
13 Social policy and employment	O	~	O
14 Energy	~	~	~
15 Industrial policy	✓	✓	✓
16 Small and medium-sized undertakings	✓	✓	✓
17 Science and research	✓	✓	✓
18 Education and training	✓	✓	✓
19 Telecommunications and information technologies	✓	~	O
20 Culture and audio-visual policy	✓	O	[✓]
21 Regional policy and co-ordination of structural instruments	~	~	~
22 Environment	~	~	O
23 Consumers and health protection	✓	✓	~
24 Co-operation in the fields of justice and home affairs	~	~	~
25 Customs union	~	~	~
26 External relations	✓	✓	✓
27 Common foreign and security policy	✓	✓	✓
28 Financial control	~	~	~
29 Financial and budgetary provisions	~	~	~
30 Institutions			
Total chapters opened	17	16	16
Total chapters provisionally closed	12	9	7

O = chapter opened, under negotiation; ✓ = chapter provisionally closed; [✓] = chapter for which the Commission has proposed provisional closure; ~ = chapter not yet opened to negotiation.

Source: European Commission (2000) Directorate-General Enlargement.

Table 2.1d State of accession negotiations with respect to chapters of the *acquis communautaire* (as of start of 2001)

Acquis chapters provisionally closed	Slovakia	Bulgaria	Romania
1 Free movement of goods	~	~	~
2 Freedom of movement for persons	~	~	~
3 Freedom to provide services	O	~	~
4 Free movement of capital	O	O	~
5 Company law	~	O	~
6 Competition policy	O	~	O
7 Agriculture	~	~	~
8 Fisheries	✓	~	~
9 Transport policy	O	~	~
10 Taxation	~	~	~
11 Economic and monetary union	~	~	~
12 Statistics	✓	✓	✓
13 Social policy and employment	~	~	~
14 Energy	~	~	~
15 Industrial policy	✓	~	~
16 Small and medium-sized undertakings	✓	✓	✓
17 Science and research	✓	✓	✓
18 Education and training	✓	✓	✓
19 Telecommunications and information technologies	O	O	O
20 Culture and audio-visual policy	✓	✓	O
21 Regional policy and co-ordination of structural instruments	~	~	~
22 Environment	~	~	~
23 Consumers and health protection	✓	✓	~
24 Co-operation in the fields of justice and home affairs	~	~	~
25 Customs union	O	~	~
26 External relations	✓	✓	✓
27 Common foreign and security policy	✓	✓	✓
28 Financial control	~	~	~
29 Financial and budgetary provisions	~	~	~
30 Institutions			
Total chapters opened	16	11	9
Total chapters provisionally closed	10	8	6

O = chapter opened, under negotiation; ✓ = chapter provisionally closed; ~ = chapter not yet opened to negotiation.

Source: European Commission (2000) Directorate-General Enlargement.

TACKLING SENSITIVE ISSUES

Each country has a set of sensitive issues that are difficult to resolve easily, both on the part of the applicant country and the EU. For example, for Hungary the question of treatment of the gypsies (classed as a minority) is an issue that has to be addressed. The Copenhagen Criteria requires that the rights of minorities have to be observed; since Hungary has some half a million gypsies their rights therefore have to be observed. Turkey is another example where its treatment of the Kurdish minority is not acceptable according to the EU standards.

SCALE OF EFFORTS TO JOIN

Some countries, such as Poland, have been slow in passing all the required laws for undertaking all the necessary reforms in order to join the EU. The case of agriculture in Poland is one example. Polish politicians are reluctant to cut the current subsidies because such a measure would be unpopular and so the politicians, themselves being under political pressure, are not willing to introduce it. Issues like these are discussed in the individual chapters for each country.

TIMING OF ACCESSION

To provide a timeframe for EU accession, it is appropriate to bring together in this study the views of each side involved in the process.

The decision makers involved in accession

The decision makers involved in the process of accession can be summarized as:

- the applicant countries;
- the decision makers of the EU:
  - the negotiators working from the European Commission
  - the decision makers of the European Council who make the ultimate decision whether or not to accept any new applicant country into the EU. This group's decision is in turn based both on the reports and recommendations of the Commission as well as each country's own internal assessment of the suitability of the applicant countries. In other words, each EU member country makes its own internal judgement on the eligibility of an applicant country.

The Nice Treaty as a precondition for enlargement

The Treaty of Nice (explained at length in Chapter 16) was designed to pave the way for the enlargement of the EU. Two sets of dates were chosen for the implementation of the Nice Treaty:

- 2004 was chosen for the reforms that affect the European Parliament, which in turn commences its new term of office in June 2004;

- those sets of reforms that affect the European Commission become effective in 2005, because a 'new commission' starts its term of office in 2005 (i.e. the term of the existing commissioners expires at the end of 2004, although some of them may be re-appointed for a second term of office).

The official view is that the implementation date for the Treaty (2004 and 2005) does not prevent the accession of new members at an earlier stage. The only requirement is that the Nice Treaty has to be ratified by all the national parliaments and that is expected to be completed by 2002. Normally it takes around 18 months for the Treaty to pass through all the national parliaments.

Yet the reweighting of the Qualified Majority Voting (QMV), which is an integral part of the institutional reform of the Nice Summit, does not come into effect until 1 January 2005 and is implemented thereafter. This date, however, has no bearing on the term of the commission nor the European Parliament. The system of 'qualified majority voting' is only applied by the European Council. The latter, in turn comprises only the heads of states and governments of the member states and their terms are decided within their respective national levels.

One may ask why has the date of 2005 been chosen in the first place? What is its significance? Phrased differently, why does the reformed QMV not come into force with immediate effect after it is ratified by all the national parliaments? Why did the Council not set an earlier date? This is the point at which one has to distinguish between the 'official view' and what is discussed in the 'corridors' within the Commission.

The rotating EU presidency

The EU Council presidency is a vital catalyst for the formulation of political policies and legislation.

Each member state of the EU takes it in turn to hold the presidency for a pre-determined six-month term. During this period the country chairs all the Council meetings and 'leads' in formulating the agenda during the course of the half-yearly presidency. The member state in question represents the entire EU in the course of its presidency when interacting with non-EU states.[1]

Table 2.2 presents the calendar of the rotating presidency of the EU over the years 1998 to 2003.

Table 2.2 The rotating presidency of the EU 1998–2003

Year	Term	Country
1998	First half-year	UK
	Second half-year	Austria
1999	First half-year	Germany
	Second half-year	Finland
2000	First half-year	Portugal
	Second half-year	France
2001	First half-year	Sweden
	Second half-year	Belgium
2002	First half-year	Spain
	Second half-year	Denmark
2003	First half-year	Greece

By following the current rotation arrangements it is possible to determine which member states will hold the presidency of the EU beyond that of Greece in 2003.

BACKGROUND TO IMPORTANT EU DECISIONS

Analysis of timing of accession requires an understanding of the way European institutions operate – that is, an understanding of how the 'very important' decisions by the EU are reached. An example of such a decision is the launch of Europe's single currency which took the best part of the 1990s to decide, prepare and finally introduce in 1999. Some may argue that the launch of the European Monetary Union (EMU) and the process of EU enlargement are dissimilar. However, on the scale of importance the enlargement of the EU (taking on board up to 13 countries) and the actual submergence of 11 national currencies under a single currency can be to some extent comparable. Indeed it is our view that the two events are comparable at some level.

For the launch of the euro two separate dates were set within the Maastricht Treaty: 1997 and 1999. For the first date of 1997 the member countries were not ready. That is, they were not able to comply with all the convergence criteria. The second date, 1999, was the final deadline and it was an all-or-nothing situation. If the countries were not ready then EMU would not happen.

In contrast, with the enlargement of the EU, no binding date has been set *a priori* for the accession of any country. Thus from that point of view there is no direct comparison with EMU. However, where the experience of EMU is relevant is where the countries were late with their preparation and with meeting the criteria. Equally, EU accession candidate countries can be slow or late for meeting all the Copenhagen Criteria and in particular in being able to close the chapters of the *acquis*. Accordingly, the date of 2004 for the first wave of entry can be argued to be still too ambitious to meet.

The other factor that made EMU finally materialize was the political will of all the euro-zone heads of states, especially that of Chancellor Helmut Kohl of Germany up to 27 October 1998. In the case of enlargement, there is no similar political will on the part of the heads of governments of the existing member states. While some member states, for example the UK, are interested in EU enlargement, others such as the countries bordering Central and Eastern Europe, for example Germany and Austria, are anxious about the flood of migrant labour from the East to their countries.

Moreover, member states such as Spain and Portugal are anxious about losing their existing share of the structural funds. Accordingly, they would not be keen to accelerate the enlargement process.

> *A Cohesion Fund was set up in 1993 to strengthen the structural policy. This is intended for those countries with a per capita GNP of less than 90 per cent of the Community average, i.e. Greece, Spain, Ireland and Portugal. The aim of the Cohesion Fund is to grant funds for environment and transport infrastructure projects.*[2]

Romano Prodi, the President of the EU, is one of the few major forces behind the enlargement. His term ends at the end of 2004, so he and Günter Verheugen, the existing Enlargement Commissioner, could push for some applicants to join before their terms are over.

In principle, the smaller the country (the smaller the size of the population) the less burden it is likely to impose on the EU when it joins the Union. A smaller country is, in some ways, less costly for the EU to admit as a new member relative to a larger one with a higher population. The burden created by the entry of a large and relatively poor country can be considered a burden in two respects:

- it will impose a bigger threat as far as the outward migration of its labour force is concerned;

- it will demand more financial assistance from the EU, for example demands for agricultural subsidies or requests for structural and cohesion funds; in short, it will be a net recipient of funds rather than a donor of funds to the EU.

It is worth noting that prior to the EU membership of Spain and Portugal, there was a great deal of anxiety on the part of the existing members about a flood of their migrant labour to the rest of the EU. As it turned out, this did not materialize. In fact, the reverse happened – the prosperity that ensued within Spain and Portugal induced an inward flow of ex-patriot labour back to their own countries.

Patterns of important EU decisions

Significant decisions on the process of enlargement so far have affected groups of five or six countries. For instance, the Luxembourg European Council in 1997 recommended that accession negotiations[3] should begin with a group of six in the year 1998. Again in 1999 at the Helsinki Council it was recommended that accession negotiations should commence with a group of six and Turkey was also allowed to become an official applicant. Also, the decision to launch monetary union embraced 11 countries. This demonstrates how important EU decisions tend to embrace groups of countries. Perhaps this is also partly related to the reality of efforts required on the part of member countries whose parliaments have to ratify each new treaty. Since entry of any new member state into the EU requires a treaty that has to be ratified, it is easier to ratify a group of six than to allow one or two or even three members to enter. However, ultimately, it comes down to costs and benefits of entry to the existing members.

SCENARIOS FOR EU ACCESSION

The following scenarios are envisaged, in the context of this study an examination of all the options and the progress of different applicant countries.

Accession path scenario 1

A group of five countries – Poland, Hungary, the Czech Republic, Slovenia and Malta – could join in 2004/2005. Another group of seven – Estonia, Cyprus, Bulgaria, Latvia, Lithuania, Romania and Slovakia – would join in 2007/2008. Turkey may possibly join in 2010 (but this is doubtful). Table 2.3 summarises the enlargement of the EU under this scenario.

Poland has been included in the first round (even though the country has been slow with its preparations) for the following reasons:

- First, it became evident in the course of this study that the country has a continuous presence at the European Commission and other EU institutions;
- Second, it was thought inconceivable that other applicant countries such as Hungary would be allowed to enter the EU without Poland – leaving the latter out would become a very difficult issue politically for the EU.

Table 2.3 Accession path of candidate countries: scenario 1

Date of accession	Countries
2004/2005	Poland
	Hungary
	Czech Republic
	Slovenia
	Malta
2007/2008	Cyprus
	Bulgaria
	Estonia
	Latvia
	Lithuania
	Romania
	Slovakia
2010	Turkey

Malta has also been included in the first round on the grounds that the country is very well prepared. The only sticking point hindering it from early accession is the country's concern about its property rights and the fear that the country's limited land would be bought up by the richer Northern Europeans such as the British and the Germans. However, the EU decision makers feel confident that a transition period over this issue could quite possibly be agreed. Discussions looking for a solution between Malta and the EU have occurred but no details on the actual number of years for a transition period are formalized as yet.

Accession path scenario 2

Under this scenario, a group of seven countries – Poland, Hungary, the Czech Republic, Slovenia, Cyprus, Estonia and Malta – could join in 2004/2005. Another group of five – Bulgaria, Latvia, Lithuania, Romania and Slovakia – would join in 2008. Turkey may possibly join in 2010 (but this is doubtful). Table 2.4 summarizes the enlargement of the EU under scenario 2.

Cyprus has been included in this scenario as a candidate for first-round entry into the EU in 2004/2005. The rationale behind this is that:

■ Turkey's involvement in the island and the tensions that have existed between the ethnic Greek and ethnic Turkish Cypriots can be put aside and the Greek part of the island can be admitted, leaving to one side the Turkish part;

■ it has been observed by the negotiators of other applicant countries that the southern dimension of EU expansion is accumulating force substantially – with strong support from Greece, who insists that the first wave of accession should not proceed without Cyprus, it is very probable that this Mediterranean country will indeed be one of the first to enter the EU.

Table 2.4 Accession path of candidate countries: scenario 2

Date of accession	Countries
2004/2005	Poland
	Hungary
	Czech Republic
	Slovenia
	Malta
	Estonia
	Cyprus
2008	Bulgaria
	Latvia
	Lithuania
	Romania
	Slovakia
2010	Turkey

The inclusion of Estonia for a 2004/2005 entry is envisaged for the following reason. Estonia was able to close six chapters of the *acquis* out of nine in the second half of the year 2000. These chapters were initially scheduled for closing during the Swedish presidency (held during January to June 2001). The country, thus has been advancing rapidly with satisfying the criteria for membership. Accordingly, it may severely object if it is excluded from the first round of EU entry.

Accession path scenario 3

This scenario is constructed on the grounds that the smaller economies stand a better chance of entry since they are easier to adapt. So the scenario has at least three countries – Hungary, Estonia and Slovenia – joining in the first round and could even embrace Malta in the first round.

According to this scenario three countries join in 2004/2005 (Hungary, Estonia, Slovenia), five more countries join in 2006 (Poland, the Czech Republic, Slovakia, Malta and Cyprus), four in 2007/2008 (Bulgaria, Latvia, Lithuania and Romania) and possibly Turkey in 2010. Table 2.5 summarizes the enlargement of the EU under this scenario.

Accession path scenario 4

In this scenario no country joins before at least ten are ready in 2007. Some countries are made to wait and some countries' accession is brought forward to

2007, so 12 candidate countries join in 2007 (*see* Table 2.6). Turkey joins possibly in 2010.

Table 2.5 Accession path of candidate countries: scenario 3

Date of accession	Countries
2004/2005	Hungary Estonia Slovenia
2006	Poland Czech Republic Slovakia Malta Cyprus
2008	Bulgaria Latvia Lithuania Romania
2010	Turkey

Table 2.6 Accession path of candidate countries: scenario 4

Date of accession	Countries
2007	Hungary Estonia Malta Cyprus Poland Czech Republic Bulgaria Latvia Lithuania Slovakia Slovenia Romania
2010	Turkey

Accession path scenario 5

This scenario was considered on the grounds that for political and diplomatic reasons, at times the EU does not wish to make any distinctions between the different accession countries – otherwise it creates rivalries among all the applicants. Thus this scenario is created (referred to as a 'Big Bang') whereby ten countries would join in 2005. Bulgaria and Romania would join in 2008 and Turkey possibly in 2010. This is regarded as the least likely scenario. Table 2.7 illustrates scenario 5.

Table 2.7 Accession path of candidate countries: scenario 5

Date of accession	Countries
2005	Hungary
	Estonia
	Malta
	Cyprus
	Poland
	Czech Republic
	Latvia
	Lithuania
	Slovakia
	Slovenia
2008	Bulgaria
	Romania
2010	Turkey

Commission officials maintain that no date for entry should be set *a priori*, because once a date is pre-set there is a tendency on the part of the applicants to become complacent and not to mobilize their resources to fulfil all the requirements. With a pre-assigned date the candidates tend to feel the EU is forced to accept their membership 'come what may', whereas when no prior entry date is formally agreed applicant countries tend to make all the effort needed to meet the EU entry requirements.

It is worth noting that while the EU insists on the candidates meeting all the requirements, some of the conditions that are set in the Copenhagen Criteria, in particular with regard to the chapters of the *acquis*, cannot be said to have been fully met by some of the existing EU member states.

The above argument rests upon the assumption that a first wave of countries would join the EU in the first half of 2004 – in time to include their members in the next European Parliament which is due for re-election in June 2004. Nevertheless, this line of reasoning rests on the statement of the President of the EU in November 2000, Romano Prodi, who said he and the other commissioners would do 'everything in our power to fulfil the European Parliament's request that the first wave of new members should be able to take part in the next parliamentary elections, due in June 2004'.[4] Moreover, the term of office of the commissioners of the European Commission is five years. Therefore, commissioners (including the Commissioner for Enlargement of the EU, Günter Verheugen, as well as the President of the European Commission) come to an end at the end of 2004. It is understood in many circles that both the Commission President and the Enlargement Commissioner are keen to have some new members joining the EU before their term expires in 2005.

Up until the publication of the Third Regular Report in 2000, the so-called 'front wave' candidates, such as Poland, Hungary and the Czech Republic, had been hoping to join the EU on 1 January 2003. The European Commission expects to conclude discussions with the 'front wave' countries in 2002. The 15 existing EU countries could take as long as a year and a half to ratify any accession agreement. Delays could, however, be possibly encountered even when considering an initial enlargement date of 2004. With this in mind, a probable date for an initial enlargement could be 1 January 2005.

The Commission has stated that its 'schedule is indicative and could be brought forward'. Bearing in mind the complexity of EU enlargement and that target dates for implementation by the EU are subject to change, it is likely that accession dates will be extended.

Following the European Commission's Regular Report on the applicant countries that was approved by the Commission in November 2000, it was reported in press conferences that the Commission will do all it can to enable the enlargement of the EU by mid-2004. The European Parliament had requested that the first group of candidate states should be given the opportunity to participate in the next elections of the European Parliament due in June 2004.

It is hoped that by the beginning of 2003 the EU entry requirement will be satisfied by some countries – primarily by the so-called 'front runners'. Thereafter, the accession of these countries would still have to be ratified by the parliaments of the 15 existing member countries. This process, by various estimates, could take some 18 months which in turn implies the 'front runners' would not be able to make the election of the European Parliament. Separately, the Commission has indicated that the starting date of 2004 is not set in stone and if a country is truly ready, there can be the possibility of early admission into the EU. On 6 November 2000 Poland announced that the country had brought forward the date by which it would pass all the necessary legislation in order to become eligible for joining the EU by 2003.

Some aspiring countries, for example Poland, have also stressed the need to have a date for budgetary reasons. However, it is not clear why such an accession date is needed for budgetary reasons. EU officials feel that setting any form of deadline or any form of pre-assigned time for entry is wrong, for it creates pressure for the EU to allow the applicant countries to join the EU even if they have not fully satisfied the requirements. It has been the experience of the Commission that there is always more pressure for countries to prepare well and become fully compliant if no accession date is set initially.

A fundamental difference between the forthcoming EU enlargement and the previous enlargements is the pre-accession preparation. The question is whether this will take a long time. It can be argued that the Commission can take too long and that the countries can take too long. Poland claims that it will be ready to join by 1 January 2003, but the community has not really committed itself to any date.

POTENTIAL FUTURE EU PARTNERS

The prospect for enlargement beyond the existing 13 applicant countries is looming and, indeed, is within reach.

On 24 November 2000 the EU made a pledge to assist five countries of the Western Balkans to prepare to become eventual members of the EU. These countries were:

- Croatia
- Bosnia-Herzegovina
- Federal Yugoslavia
- Macedonia
- Albania.

This pledge was made at a summit that took place in Croatia. The EU donated some 4.65 billion euros to these countries to prepare them over the period 2000–6. The aim of this aid is to help these countries to introduce democratic and economic reforms. At this summit Macedonia signed the Europe Agreement with the EU.

Beyond the above five potential candidates is a set of even more remote future prospects:

- Ukraine
- Georgia
- Moldova
- Armenia
- Azerbaijan
- Kyrgystan.

This could push the eastern borders of the EU as far as the outer rims of St Petersburg at one end and the Black Sea at the other end. However, every major exercise on this scale has its advantages and disadvantages.

Undoubtedly it will not be easy to bring on board a large number of participants from the former centrally planned economies into the EU. There will be many obstacles to overcome.

Notes

1   There has been some discussion within the EU about changing the rotation of the presidency. In some quarters there has been an unofficial suggestion about

changing the current six-month term to a one-year term. Advocates of change maintain that the existing presidency rotation is very inefficient. In fact, they go as far as calling it a 'circus'. But such a change may cause a negative reaction from some member states.

2   From the European Commission.

3   Luxembourg European Council (1997), *Presidency Conclusions*, December.

4   *Financial Times* (2000) 'Brussels sets 2004 date for EU enlargement – "Road map for negotiations" receives broad welcome from candidates', 9 November.

Part two

3

Poland

OVERVIEW

Poland's relationship with the EU dates back to 1988 when it first signed its free trade agreement (*see* Table 3.2). However, the country formally began its accession negotiations in March 1998. In some circles Poland holds a pivotal role in the EU enlargement, in that it is considered inconceivable that any new member (or members) would be admitted to the EU without Poland. On the other hand, the authorities responsible for the negotiations and admission of new member states rule out this scenario. They maintain that in principle any new member or group of members that have satisfied all the EU requirements for entry will be able to join regardless of Poland's position. (In other words, enlargement of the EU can proceed with or without Poland.)

Poland has the highest population among the EU applicant countries and some argue that it may entail the highest cost for the EU if the country is not fully ready for accession. Indeed Poland has made major strides in the transformation from a centrally planned economy to a liberalized market economy. Table 3.1 provides an overview of the Polish economy.

Table 3.1 Overview of the Polish economy

Population average (millions)(1999)[1]	38.654
Gross Domestic Product(GDP)(per capita at current prices)(US$)(2000)[2]	4,043
GDP per capita (Purchasing Power Standards* in euros)(as of end 1999)[1]	7,806
GDP per capita (Purchasing Power Standards)(per cent of EU average)(1999)[1]	37
GDP at current prices (billion euros)(1999)[1]	146
Inflation rate, annual average (September 2000**)[1]	10.4
Appreciation/depreciation of national currency against the euro/Ecu (2001) (1997=100)[3]	92.52

Sources: [1] Eurostat (2000); [2] IMF (2000) *World Economic Outlook Database*, September; [3] Datastream.

Notes: * Eurostat defines Purchasing Power Standards as an artificial currency to enable correct comparison of volume of goods and services produced by different countries. Figures have been calculated using the population figures from National Accounts, which may differ from those used in demographic statistics.
** Moving 12-month average rate of change.

PROCESS OF EU ACCESSION

The Europe Agreement that Poland signed with the EU in December 1991 came into effect in February 1994. Poland officially applied for EU membership in April 1994. The country was included with Hungary, Estonia, the Czech Republic, Slovenia and Cyprus in the first round of accession negotiations recommended by the 1997 Luxembourg European Council. The actual negotiations commenced in March 1998. Table 3.2 gives a summary of the accession process.

Table 3.2 Evolution of the relationship between Poland and the EU

Date	Stage of application	Additional comments
1988	Free Trade Agreements	Partial liberalization of trade started relationships between the EEC and former COMECON countries
December 1991	Europe Agreement signed	The legal basis for the relations with the EU
February 1994	Europe Agreement came into force	
April 1994	Official application for EU membership submitted	
March 1998	Accession negotiations began	
April 1998	Analytical examination of the *acquis* for Poland began	Concluded in autumn 1999
October 1998	The Commission issued its first Regular Report on Poland	Aimed at Vienna European Council
October 1999	The Commission issued its second Regular Report on Poland	Aimed at Helsinki European Council
December 1999	An amended Accession Partnership was adopted	
February 2000	Update of the screening exercise began	Takes into account the new *acquis* that had been adopted in March 1998
April 2000	Poland presented an amended National Programme for the Adoption of the *Acquis* (NPAA)	
November 2000	The Commission issued its third Regular Report on Poland	

Sources: European Commission (2000) *Regular Report on Poland's Progress Towards Accession*, November; European Commission (1999) *Accession Partnership for Poland*, Directorate-General Enlargement, December.

Poland was one of the earliest countries in Central and Eastern Europe to embark on economic and political transformation (from a socialist republic with a planned economy to a democracy with a market economy). This, coupled with a strong political will to move ahead with reforms, underlined Poland's early success with macroeconomic stabilization, restructuring and democratization of society. Its economic integration and political and social convergence with Western Europe proceeded at a rapid rate, and in April 1994 Poland became one of the first former socialist countries to apply for a membership of the EU. In the early years of the drive towards accession, Poland became a leading partner among a number of countries aspiring to become EU member states.

Agriculture is a problem area for Poland with respect to EU accession. Poland wishes to have all the advantages of the Common Agricultural Policy (CAP) – especially for cereal. However, the way its agricultural sector is structured, it does not conform to that of the EU. Poland's definition of a 'farmer' differs from that of the EU. A 'farmer' in the definition of the EU is one that produces for the consumption of others and does not produce just for himself or herself. The European Commission has estimated that roughly 30 per cent of the population of Poland are in the latter category – i.e. they produce only for their own and their family's consumption. This could impose a big burden on EU as far as agricultural subsidies are concerned. Poland has to modernize itself substantially in this sector.

For some products (mainly meat and milk) the Poles wish to be given a period of grace until 2006 to undertake the necessary reforms. But Poland does not wish to call it a transitional period – so that it would not jeopardise its ability to receive agricultural subsidies from the EU under the CAP.

MEETING EU REQUIREMENTS FOR ENTRY

Poland has been attempting to meet all the requirements of the Copenhagen Agreement, which was signed in 1993. However, the country is not as yet fully in compliance with all these conditions. These are explained further below.

Meeting political criteria

With respect to the political criteria the areas that require further action are:

- reform of the judiciary for the full compliance with the acquis;
- measures to eradicate corruption and the introduction of the necessary laws and regulations;
- efforts to ensure equal opportunities.

The above measures have to accelerate in order to ensure full compliance before entry into the EU.

Meeting economic criteria

Poland is close to meeting the economic criteria.[1] However, there are some areas that need further action:

- The equilibrium between demand and supply is now largely established, but the Government still influences prices for electricity, central heating, transportation, pharmaceutical and telecommunication services.

- There are still barriers to market exit. The bankruptcy system needs to be changed in favour of creditors.

- The legal system is in place and property rights are guaranteed, but a certain degree of bureaucracy obstructs business activity.

- Macroeconomic instability still exists in terms of external and public finances.

- The current account deficit is increasing and in turn placing pressure on Poland's economic policy.

- Since 1998 the level of unemployment has increased steadily and the control of inflation is proving to be difficult. Public finances are characterized by a high number of extra-budgetary funds that obstruct an efficient public expenditure management.

There is a broad political consensus in Poland on the conduct of economic policy. Nevertheless, there are still divergances on some reforms that have been delaying the government decision process.

Meeting obligations of membership

After receiving a strong reprimand from the European Commission in mid-1999 on the rate of adoption of the EU legislation, Poland attempted to create a special Parliamentary Committee on European Law. This has substantially enhanced the capability of the country in taking on board the *acquis* (the rules and regulations of the EU). However, further improvements in strengthening the administrative capacity for adopting and implementing it are required.

As of the start of the year 2001 Poland has provisionally closed 13 chapters of the *acquis* (*see* Table 3.3).

TIMING OF ACCESSION

Of the three principle requirements for entry, Poland, in principle, satisfies the political and economic citeria. However, within each category there remain areas of concern that need to be addressed. Yet, none of these yardsticks set for assessing the eligibility of a country for membership are quantified so that one could assess it. On a scale of 10, say, Poland scores 4 or 5.

Table 3.3 Poland: state of negotiations on chapters of the *acquis communautaire* (at start of 2001)

Chapter	Title	State of play	Date
1	Free movement of goods	[✓]	
2	Freedom of movement for persons	O	
3	Freedom to provide services	✓	Nov. 2000
4	Free movement of capital	O	
5	Company law	O	
6	Competition policy	O	
7	Agriculture	O	
8	Fisheries	O	
9	Transport policy	O	
10	Taxation	O	
11	Economic and monetary union	✓	Dec. 1999
12	Statistics	✓	June 1999
13	Social policy and employment	O	
14	Energy	O	
15	Industrial policy	✓	June 1999
16	Small and medium-sized undertakings	✓	Nov. 1998
17	Science and research	✓	Nov. 1998
18	Education and training	✓	Nov. 1998
19	Telecommunications and information technologies	✓	June 1999
20	Culture and audio-visual policy	✓	Nov. 2000
21	Regional policy and co-ordination of structural instruments	O	
22	Environment	O	
23	Consumers and health protection	✓	June 1999
24	Co-operation in the fields of justice and home affairs	O	
25	Customs union	O	
26	External relations	✓	Dec. 1999
27	Common foreign and security policy	✓	June 2000
28	Financial control	✓	June 2000
29	Financial and budgetary provisions	O	
30	Institutions		
31	Other		
Total chapters opened		29	(Start of 2001)
Total chapters provisionally closed		13	(Start of 2001)

O = chapter opened, under negotiation; ✓ = chapter provisionally closed; [✓] = chapter for which the Commission has proposed provisional closure.

Source: European Commission (2000) Directorate-General Enlargement.

The only area where there is a quantifiable measure is with the third requirement – meeting the obligations of membership. However, one should not interpret the number of the *acquis* chapters closed as a barometer indicating how prepared a country is.

Originally Poland set itself a timetable to complete its negotiations with the EU by the first half of 2001 – hoping to conclude the bulk of the negotiations in 2000. As it turned out, this schedule did not materialize, since Poland had only managed to satisfy 13 chapters of the *acquis*. However, on 6 November 2000 Poland expressed its strong commitment to pass all the necessary legislation by 2001 (in order to become eligible for joining the EU by 2003). This agenda seems both ambitious and unlikely. Realistically viewing the accession date, even if the formal negotiations with the EU may finish by the end of 2002, it normally takes 18 months for the EU governments to ratify any agreement reached by the European Council. Therefore the accession of any candidate country, including Poland, is unlikely to be before June 2004 which is the date for the elections of the European Parliament.

The different scenarios considered for the timing of Poland's entry into the EU are discussed at length in Chapter 2.

The prominent role that Poland has played in fostering the process of liberalization of Central and Eastern Europe and also in bringing forth the issue of enlargement makes the country a key candidate, whose importance cannot be ignored. On these grounds it could be a strong candidate for early accession.

Note

1   European Commission (2000), *Regular Report on Poland's Progress Towards Accession*, November, pp. 22–31.

Hungary

OVERVIEW

Hungary appears to be one of the most eligible states (if not the most eligible state) for joining the EU. Starting from a position of considerable strength, the country has made a substantial effort in preparing for its EU accession.

The Hungarian economy[1] has undergone a radical process of privatization, which is an important requirement in the accession process. As a result, Hungary's ability to compete on an international level is greatly enhanced. By the end of the 1990s the privatization process was approaching its conclusion, with over 80 per cent of Gross Domestic Product generated by the private sector.[2] It is clear that a large segment of the economy is permanently exposed to market forces. Table 4.1 provides some insights into the structure of the economy.

Table 4.1 Overview of the Hungarian economy

Population average (millions)(1999)[1]	10.068
Gross Domestic Product(GDP)(per capita at current prices)(US$)(1999)[2]	5,238
GDP per capita (Purchasing Power Standards* in euros)(as of end 1999)[1]	10,705
GDP per capita (Purchasing Power Standards)(per cent of EU average)(1999)[1]	51
GDP at current prices (billion euros)(1999)[1]	45.4
Inflation rate, annual average (as of June 2000**)[1]	10.2
Appreciation/depreciation of national currency against the euro/Ecu (2001) (1997=100)[3]	76.59

Sources: [1] Eurostat (2000); [2] IMF (2000) *World Economic Outlook Database*, September; [3] Datastream.

Notes: * Eurostat defines Purchasing Power Standards as an artificial currency to enable correct comparison of volume of goods and services produced by different countries. Figures have been calculated using the population figures from National Accounts, which may differ from those used in demographic statistics.
** Moving 12-month average rate of change.

Hungary also has the confidence of direct investors from abroad. Examples of the foreign companies that have penetrated the Hungarian economy and have brought a large volume of foreign capital to the country include Audi, Philips, IBM, Suzuki, GM and Ford. Domestic firms have also found the reform from state ownership a fruitful process, with the former government telecoms firm Matav performing to levels that are almost comparable to those of the EU.

The financial sector has been developing rapidly (in line with EU entry requirements), as has the insurance sector. However, to meet the EU standards fully, there is still a need for Hungary to strengthen regulation, particularly for those companies that operate across a number of areas in the market (such as pension providers).[3]

PROCESS OF EU ACCESSION

Hungary applied to join the EU in March 1994 and the European Council of Ministers decided that the country could open discussions with the European Commission in April 1995.[4] In July 1997 the Commission presented a judgement to the Council in which it was suggested that formal discussions for entry could commence with Hungary.[5] The pre-accession strategy set out a programme that focused on the issues that had to take precedence, and a timetable regarding these issues.[6] In its progress report on Hungary published in November 2000, the European Commission was very complimentary about Hungary's endeavours to meet its obligations for EU membership.

Table 4.2 gives a brief chronology of Hungary's process of EU accession.

Table 4.2 Evolution of the relationship between Hungary and the EU

Date	Stage of application	Additional comments
December 1991	Europe Agreement signed[1]	A bilateral trade agreement with the European Economic Area
February 1994	Europe Agreement came into effect[1]	
March 1994	Hungary presented its application for EU membership[1]	
18 April 1995	EU Council of Ministers implemented consultation on membership[2]	
December 1997	Council reached agreement on the procedures for accession negotiations[1]	
July 1997	The Commission submitted its Opinion on Hungary's application to the European Council[3]	
March 1998	Accession Negotiations began[1]	
April 1998	Analytical examination of the acquis for Hungary began[3]	Concluded in autumn 1999
October 1998	The Commission issued its first Regular Report on Hungary	Aimed at Vienna European Council
October 1999	The Commission issued its second Regular Report on Hungary	Aimed at Helsinki European Council
February 2000	Update of the screening exercise began[3]	Included the new acquis that had been adopted in March 1998
November 2000	The Commission issued its third Regular Report on Hungary	

Sources: [1] European Commission (2000), Directorate-General Enlargement; [2] European Commission (1997) Commission Opinion on Hungary's Application for Membership of the European Union, July; [3] European Commission (2000), Regular Report on Hungary's Progress Towards Accession, November.

MEETING EU REQUIREMENTS FOR ENTRY

In relation to the requirements set out in the Copenhagen Criteria, Hungary has performed well during the 1990s. This section will state whether specific requirements for EU entry are being met and what needs to be done in the future.

Meeting political criteria

With regard to the political criteria, Hungary's institutions operate with relative efficiency and elections are performed in a climate of democracy. For example, local elections have been successfully held three times since 1989.

The subject of minority representation is still a debated point. To continue with the progress made in democracy and the rule of law, Hungary has adopted a programme to develop further public administration. This involves putting in place a level of devolution in the regions and bringing about improved working conditions for public sector employees.[7]

The political stability of Hungary during 1998–2000 deteriorated, even though overall progress since 1989 has been very good. These political problems are causing the EU concern and may jeopardize Hungary's rapid accession to the Union.

It has been suggested in a report by the International Press Institute (1999) that the Hungarian press lacks transparency and accountability.[8] This would certainly seem to be the case considering that the board for the Hungarian Television Public Foundation is comprised of only government representatives. Furthermore the report describes how in some instances journalists have been subjected to physical assault.[9] The problem of media control needs to be seen as a significant issue in Hungary's attempts at EU accession, particularly as it is an important issue for citizens.

The Hungarian judicial system is functioning well and has shown good progress, especially on legal training. In 1998 some 500 judges were involved in the training programmes on EU law, and it is expected that they will also undertake postgraduate courses on the subject.[10]

With regard to human and minority rights, the situation of the minority Roma is of most concern and has been identified as a definite problem for Hungary's accession. There is evidence that the Roma are not being treated fairly. Examples include:

■ the isolation of the children of the Roma group from other children in Hungarian schools;

■ discrimination observed on the part of the police and a general feeling of prejudice.[11]

The Government is taking steps to rectify this situation. For example in May 1999 it introduced a measure – the 'Government Decision 1047/1999 (V.5.) Korm' – to improve the habitat conditions and social standing of the Roma.[12] In line with EU requirements that such decisions are practised in daily life, the Government has set goals for the relevant government organizations. Each of the ministries is required to assign a part of its budget to meet the government decision, while the central budget will also provide funds.[13]

Another area of concern with regard to Hungary's accession to the EU is related to the element of corruption. The Government has to take some steps to rectify the situation.

Meeting economic criteria

By and large Hungary meets the economic criteria as part of the Copenhagen Criteria. However, concerns still remain in satisfying parts of economic conditions. The areas of concern are listed below:

1   Controlled prices still form 18 per cent of the retail price index. Prices are regulated for:

- certain energy prices
- pharmaceuticals
- local government housing rents
- public transport
- telephone tariffs.

2   The level of inflation (standing at around 9.6 per cent in the summer of 2000) has to be brought further down. Between 1997 and 1999 inflation dropped from 18.3 per cent to 10.0 per cent. Despite the falling levels of inflation, the figures still exceed official predictions.[14]

3   As far as sustainable public finances are concerned, rail transport, the health system and local governments are a burden on public funds. They require modernization and restructuring.[15]

4   Doubts still remain about the integrity of the organization responsible for supervision of the financial sector. The pension system also requires further reforms.[16]

Meeting obligations of membership

Hungary's progress in applying the chapters of the *acquis* is shown in Table 4.3. The country has provisionally closed 14 chapters of the *acquis*. In terms of number of chapters closed, this puts Hungary on a par with Slovenia.

Table 4.3 Hungary: state of negotiations on chapters of the *acquis communautaire* (at start of 2001)

Chapter	Title	State of play	Date
1	Free movement of goods	O	
2	Freedom of movement for persons	O	
3	Freedom to provide services	O	
4	Free movement of capital	O	
5	Company law	O	
6	Competition policy	O	
7	Agriculture	O	
8	Fisheries	✓	June 2000
9	Transport policy	O	
10	Taxation	O	
11	Economic and monetary union	✓	Dec. 1999
12	Statistics	✓	June 2000
13	Social policy and employment	✓	Nov. 2000
14	Energy	✓	Nov. 2000
15	Industrial policy	✓	June 2000
16	Small and medium-sized undertakings	✓	Nov. 1998
17	Science and research	✓	Nov. 1998
18	Education and training	✓	Nov. 1998
19	Telecommunications and information technologies	✓	June 2000
20	Culture and audio-visual policy	O	
21	Regional policy and co-ordination of structural instruments	O	
22	Environment	O	
23	Consumers and health protection	✓	June 1999
24	Co-operation in the fields of justice and home affairs	O	
25	Customs union	O	
26	External relations	✓	Nov. 2000
27	Common foreign and security policy	✓	June 2000
28	Financial control	✓	June 2000
29	Financial and budgetary provisions	O	
30	Institutions		
31	Other		
Total chapters opened		29	(Start of 2001)
Total chapters provisionally closed		14	(Start of 2001)

O = chapter opened, under negotiation; ✓ = chapter provisionally closed.

Source: European Commission (2000) Directorate-General Enlargement.

TIMING OF ACCESSION

Hungary aims to have put in place all the 'internal preconditions' for accession by the close of 2002.[17] However, the earliest date the country could possibly enter would not be before 2004, so that it might be able to have representatives in the European Parliament (due for election in June 2004).

The reforms made by the Nice Treaty to the European Parliament also come into effect in 2004. However, the reweighting of the qualified majority voting within the European Council does not come into effect before 2005. The official EU view is that the implementation dates for the Nice Summit do not preclude earlier entry by the applicant countries. Yet, behind the scene, the private view points towards the first round of accession not materializing before 2004/2005.

For Hungary, however, the European Commission, still identifies the prevalence of corruption as a serious problem. Indeed, the magnitude of the problem in the country should not be underestimated. Needless to say, the element of corruption permeates throughout Central and Eastern Europe, and Hungary is no exception. Nevertheless, Hungary cannot be complacent in this respect and has to foster a political environment that is more in tune with the EU.

Notes

1   European Economics and Financial Centre (1999) *Economic and Financial Review*, (6)4, Winter.

2   European Commission (1999) *Hungary's Progress Towards Accession – 1999 Regular Report from the Commission*, October.

3   Ibid.

4   European Commission (1997) *Commission Opinion on Hungary's Application for Membership of the European Union*, 15 July.

5   European Commission (1998) *Accession Partnership for Hungary*, March.

6   Ibid.

7   European Commission (1999) *Regular Report on Hungary's Progress Towards Accession*, October.

8   European Parliament White Paper (2000) *European Parliament Secretariat Working Party Task Force 'Enlargement', Briefing No. 2: Hungary and the Enlargement of the European Union*, 19 April, Luxembourg.

9   Ibid.

10 European Commission (1999), *Regular Report on Hungary's Progress towards Accession*, October.

11 European Parliament White Paper (2000) *European Parliament Secretariat Working Party Task Force 'Enlargement', Briefing No. 2: Hungary and the Enlargement of the European Union*, 19 April, Luxembourg.

12 Hungarian National Plan for the Adoption of the *Acquis* (2000) *Political Criteria*.

13 Ibid.

14 Pudschedl (2000) Bank of Austria: *Bright Sunshine CEE Report* 2/200.

15 European Commission (2000) *Regular Report on Hungary's Progress Towards Accession*, November.

16 Ibid.

17 Republic of Hungary Ministry of Foreign Affairs Spokesman's Office (2000) *Joint Statement of the Parties represented in the National Assembly of the Republic of Hungary and of the Government on the current issues of the accession process*, September.

5

Czech Republic

OVERVIEW

In the mid-1990s the Czech Republic was perceived as the most eligible of the countries of Central and Eastern Europe aspiring to join the EU. The Czechs' eligibility was mainly on macroeconomic grounds. At that time the country could even meet most of the criteria laid down for joining the European Monetary Union.

With a national debt to GDP ratio (at the time) of around 16 per cent, a public-sector budget surplus and a low inflation, the Czech Republic during that period was far ahead of many of the existing members of the EU, who could not satisfy most of the Maastricht Criteria. Nevertheless, the financial crises that hit the Czech economy during May 1997 set the country back in meeting a number of EU requirements for entry. The country experienced a substantial run on its currency. This turmoil almost paralyzed the Czech financial system and banks found it almost impossible to lend even to established reputable companies. Subsequently the banking sector had to undergo considerable restructuring. Table 5.1 provides some insights into the Czech economy.

Table 5.1 Overview of the economy of the Czech Republic

Population average (millions)(1999)[1]	10.283
Gross Domestic Product(GDP)(per capita at current prices)(US$)(1999)[2]	5,177
GDP per capita (Purchasing Power Standards* in euros)(as of end 1999)[1]	12,498
GDP per capita (Purchasing Power Standards)(per cent of EU average)(1999)[1]	59
GDP at current prices (billion euros)(1999)[1]	49.8
Inflation rate, annual average (September 2000**)[1]	3.3
Appreciation/depreciation of national currency against the euro/Ecu (2001) (1997=100)[3]	96.35

Sources: [1] Eurostat (2000); [2] IMF (2000) World Economic Outlook Database, September; [3] Datastream.

Notes: * Eurostat defines Purchasing Power Standards as an artificial currency to enable correct comparison of volume of goods and services produced by different countries. Figures have been calculated using the population figures from National Accounts, which may differ from those used in demographic statistics.
** Moving 12-month average rate of change.

The creation of the Czech Securities Commission and its hard-line stance on disclosure requirements has to some extent been able to redress the problem of market risk. Furthermore, a Revitalization Agency was established in October 1999, which was administrated by a team comprising a US investment bank as well as a UK private equity group. With this structure in place, it is hoped that significant benefits can be received by a number of companies (mainly with large debts to state-owned banks) which will be recapitalized, restructured and then sold to strategic investors.

Since the 1990 elections, which could be defined as a referendum against the communist regime, the Czech political complexion has been characterized by democracy.

The Czech economy has been under pressure to construct an enforceable legal system that includes the regulation of property rights. In so doing, it was hoped that the country could facilitate a degree of consensus about transparency of prices and the essentials of economic policy required for the pursuit of macroeconomic stability.

Public opinion in the Czech Republic is in favour of EU enlargement, which is seen as a very positive step. The benefits of joining a large economic union will not only enhance trade but will also be a testament to the success of the economic transformation the Czech Republic has made from a command to a market economy.

PROCESS OF EU ACCESSION

Membership of the EU is considered by the Czech Republic as a source of consolidation of their newly born democracy and enhancement of their international security. Table 5.2 gives an account of the stages of the relationship of the Czech Republic with the European Union on its path to EU entry and pages 64–67 present the state of Czech compliance with the entry requirement.

Table 5.2 Evolution of the relationship between the Czech Republic and the EU

Date	Stage of application	Additional comments
October 1993	Europe Agreement signed	The 'Europe Agreement' is a bilateral trade agreement between the European Community and the Czech Republic
February 1995	Europe Agreement came into force	
January 1996	Official application for EU membership submitted	
31 March 1998	Accession negotiations began	
March 1998	First Accession Partnerships decided between the European Commission and the Czech Republic	Set out short and medium-term strategies and priorities as they pertain to the Acquis
April 1998	Analytical examination of the acquis for the Czech Republic began	
October 1998	The European Commission issued its first Regular Report on the Czech Republic	Aimed at Vienna European Council The Regular Reports give an overview of development

Date	Stage of application	Additional comments
May 1999	The Czech Republic presented an amended National Programme for the Adoption of the *Acquis* (NPAA)	Established a schedule for meeting the goals set out in the Accession Partnerships
May 1999	Analytical examination of the *acquis* for Estonia completed	
October 1999	The Commission issued its second Regular Report on the Czech Republic	Aimed at Helsinki European Council
December 1999	An amended Accession Partnership adopted	
February 2000	Update of the screening exercise began	
June 2000	The Czech Republic presented an amended National Programme for the Adoption of the *Acquis* (NPAA)	
November 2000	The Commission issued its third Regular Report on the Czech Republic	

Sources: European Commission (2000) *Regular Report on the Czech Republic's Progress Towards Accession*, November; European Commission (1999) *Accession Partnership for the Czech Republic*, Directorate-General Enlargement, December.

With respect to trade, reorientation in the post-communism years of the Czech Republic has seen the closer integration of trade with the West, in particular with Germany. The EU as a whole took 69 per cent of Czech exports in 1998 and supplied 58 per cent of imports.[1] However, even here there is another caveat. In 1993 following the split of Czechoslovakia, both the Czech Republic and Slovakia entered into a customs union agreement allowing for the free flow of goods and services. With both countries at different stages in EU accession, the potential ramifications of this on the obligations of EU membership, including the unambiguous support of EU policy, has created disquiet among EU officials.

The desire of the two candidates to maintain the union is viewed within the EU as a direct affront and potential threat to its common trade zone. Prior to 1999, the Czech Government forwarded a request for a compromise whereby Slovakia is offered membership alongside the Czech Republic. However, at that time both the EU's Commissioner for Foreign Politics, Hans van den Brooke, and Germany's then EU Minister, Günter Verheugen (now European Commissioner for Enlargement), suggested that the continuation of the union would prove detrimental to Czech admittance into the EU.

The analytical examination of the *acquis* (screening) for the Czech Republic started in April 1998 and concluded in May 1999 with the examination of the chapter on financial and budgetary provisions. An update of the screening started at the beginning of 2000.

MEETING EU REQUIREMENTS FOR ENTRY

The Czech Republic has obligated itself to comply with all the membership criteria as well as meeting, implementing and enforcing all the requirements as stated in the *acquis communautaire*. However, the Czech Republic was disappointed with the Commission Regular Report (2000) which put the country's progress rather behind some of the other applicant countries.

The Czech Republic has provisionally satisfied 13 of the 29 chapters of the *acquis communautaire* that it has had opened. This places it behind Hungary, Poland and Estonia in terms of chapters of the *acquis* provisionally closed. Estonia has in fact satisfied 16 *acquis* chapters.

Meeting political criteria

Overall, the Czech Republic meets the political criteria. However, more work is needed in the following areas:

- the justice system;
- the fight against discrimination towards the Roma minority;
- irradication of corruption;
- elimination of financial illegalities.

The following points of concern remain:

- The country is moving towards implementing an effective legal structure for local government. However, in the areas of public administration and the judiciary, not enough has been done to fulfil the requirements of the short and medium-term strategy outlined in the Accession Partnership document published by the Commission. While some work has been completed, other vital steps are not yet visible. It is vital that restructuring is undertaken in these areas so that the *acquis* and the democratic system can be upheld.

- Sufficient progress has not yet been made to combat corruption. If this area is rectified there will be an increase in public and business confidence.

- Human liberties are acknowledged, as they have been in the past, and the Government has taken account of these issues when it has undertaken reforms. Areas that still need addressing are overcrowded prisons and the trade in women and children.

■ Noticeable progress has been made with the Roma, especially concerning their education. If this is to be made permanent, however, progress has to continue in the future, especially to satisfy the demands of the 'Accession Partnership' criteria.

Meeting economic criteria

The Czech Republic is generally managing to meet the economic requirements set out by the European Council in Copenhagen in June 1993.[2] Macroeconomic stability has been reached in terms of price stability and a stable external account.
   There are, however, some areas that still require further action:

■ Barriers to market entry and exit are still present.

■ The Czech Republic needs better bankruptcy procedures. The legislation is obsolete and improvements in the court system are needed, especially with the effective application of the amendment to the Bankruptcy Law and the new Law on Public Auctions that were entered in May 2000.

■ There is macroeconomic instability in terms of public finance.

■ Public finances need to be sustained in the medium term. While the strategy for privatization is acceptable, it has to be improved without delay.

■ There is an undeveloped financial sector.

■ There is still a lack of transparency in the capital market and price manipulation is commonplace. The fragmented security market leads to a continuous presence of different prices for the same stock. The capital market remains a poor source of funding for the private sector.

■ The weak legal system has encouraged the development of some illegal business practices.

■ There is a lack of supervisory bodies to fight financial irregularities.

■ There is a need for better co-operation between the police and the courts.

The Czech Republic's minority government and its opposition party are in general consensus over economic policies.

Meeting obligations of membership

Since March 1998, when the accession negotiations first formally began, 13 chapters (of the 29 opened thus far) have been provisionally closed (*see* Table 5.3). These chapters have been concerned with science and research, education and training, small and medium-sized enterprises, statistics, industrial policy, telecommunications, fisheries, consumer protection, free movement of goods, customs union, external relations, common foreign and security policy, and European Monetary Union. Negotiations continue for the remaining chapters.

Table 5.3 Czech Republic: state of negotiations on chapters of the *acquis communautaire* (at start of 2001)

Chapter	Title	State of play	Date
1	Free movement of goods	✓	Dec. 1999
2	Freedom of movement for persons	O	
3	Freedom to provide services	O	
4	Free movement of capital	O	
5	Company law	O	
6	Competition policy	O	
7	Agriculture	O	
8	Fisheries	✓	June 1999
9	Transport policy	O	
10	Taxation	O	
11	Economic and monetary union	✓	Dec. 1999
12	Statistics	✓	June 1999
13	Social policy and employment	O	
14	Energy	O	
15	Industrial policy	✓	June 1999
16	Small and medium-sized undertakings	✓	Nov. 1998
17	Science and research	✓	Nov. 1998
18	Education and training	✓	Nov. 1998
19	Telecommunications and information technologies	✓	June 1999
20	Culture and audio-visual policy	O	
21	Regional policy and co-ordination of structural instruments	O	
22	Environment	O	
23	Consumers and health protection	✓	June 1999
24	Co-operation in the fields of justice and home affairs	O	
25	Customs union	✓	June 1999
26	External relations	✓	June 1999
27	Common foreign and security policy	✓	June 1999
28	Financial control	O	
29	Financial and budgetary provisions	O	
30	Institutions		
31	Other		
Total chapters opened		29	(Start of 2001)
Total chapters provisionally closed		13	(Start of 2001)

O = chapter opened, under negotiation; ✓ = chapter provisionally closed.

Source: European Commission (2000) Directorate-General Enlargement.

TIMING OF ACCESSION

The timing of accession for the Czech Republic resembles that of Poland, in that the country may or may not be in the first round of new memberships. That is, if the first round occurs in 2004 and takes in a very small number of countries, it is possible that the Czech Republic would not be included. The number of the *acquis* chapters that the country has provisionally closed (13 out of 31) and the fact that the European Commission has placed its progress behind some of the others, hinders the Czech Republic somewhat in early entry. Equally, the Czech Republic was not too happy with the way the Commission expressed its concern about its progress.

With the current tentative 'roadmap' indicated by the European Commission, any entry before 2004 is more or less ruled out. Thus, with this agenda ahead, if the Czech Republic does not speed up its preparations and its reforms, the earliest time of entry could be 2005 or 2006. On the other hand the country could make a serious attempt not to fall behind and catch up with its fellow accession partners. The two issues of its customs union with Slovakia and the transition period it is seeking for restricting its land ownership could prove stumbling blocks and will have to be resolved.

Notes

1 European Parliament (2000) *Briefing No. 4: The Czech Republic and the Enlargement of the European Union.*

2 European Commission (2000) *Regular Report on the Czech Republic's Progress Towards Accession*, November, pp. 28–37.

6

Estonia

OVERVIEW

Estonia is generally regarded as a front-runner for EU accession. It can be argued that has been a big achievement for the country to reach this position. In 1991 Estonia declared its independence, severed all administrative relations with Moscow and introduced a new system of independent governance. Subsequently the country launched a process of transformation into a market economy. Indeed, Estonia has been one of the most progressive of transition economies in Eastern Europe.

In 1991 Estonia replaced its Soviet-style turnover tax with a value-added tax (VAT).[1] In 1992 Estonia also adopted what proved to be a very successful strategy by re-introducing the old Estonian currency, the kroon, and installing a currency board by anchoring the kroon to the Deutschmark at 8 kroons per Deutschmark, an arrangement that Estonia has managed to maintain quite successfully. Moreover, inflation in Estonia did not spiral out of control.

During the 1990s, Estonia enjoyed a low and falling inflation rate,[2] largely due to its tight fiscal policy and currency board arrangement. The latter added particular credibility to Estonia's economic policies by limiting the discretionary power of the monetary authorities. By mid-1994 almost all prices, except for a few public services, were freed from administrative control. Distribution of state property and assets was done through a voucher-based privatization programme (i.e. vouchers were sold to citizens which were then exchanged for shares in privatized companies). Estonia's voucher-based privatization programme proved to be one of the more successful in Central and Eastern Europe.

Estonia was for a long time one of the best performing countries in Eastern Europe. Its economy suffered, however, when in 1998 Russia defaulted on its payments to the International Monetary Fund (IMF). Table 6.1 provides some insights into the basic characteristics of the Estonian economy.

Table 6.1 Overview of the Estonian economy

Population average (millions)(1999)[1]	1.442
Gross Domestic Product(GDP)(per capita at current prices)(US$)(2000)[2]	3,893
GDP per capita (Purchasing Power Standards* in euros)(as of end 1999)[1]	7,682
GDP per capita (Purchasing Power Standards)(per cent of EU average)(1999)[1]	36
GDP at current prices (billion euros)(1999)[1]	4.8
Inflation rate, annual average (June 2000**)[1]	3.7
Appreciation/depreciation of national currency against the euro/Ecu (2001) (1997=100)[3]	98.86

Sources: [1] Eurostat (2000); [2] IMF (2000) *World Economic Outlook Database*, September; [3] Datastream.

Notes: * Eurostat defines Purchasing Power Standards as an artificial currency to enable correct comparison of volume of goods and services produced by different countries. Figures have been calculated using the population figures from National Accounts, which may differ from those used in demographic statistics.
** Moving 12-month average rate of change.

PROCESS OF EU ACCESSION

From the outset Estonia pursued a policy of widespread liberalization of market forces in order to secure a more rapid and comprehensive transition from the previous planned economy.

Post liberalization, some sweeping liberalization measures were pursued by Estonia. Among these were:

- fiscal restructuring, including the introduction of value-added tax;
- price liberalization, which occurred very soon following independence and was almost completed by 1994, when most prices were liberalized except for a few public services;
- privatization;
- trade liberalization – the complete abolishment of trade tariffs and small subsidies to the agricultural sector;
- opening borders to foreign direct investment.

One of the first steps that Estonia took at the start of its transition was to open its borders to trade. Estonia's policy of no tariffs on trade and the lowest subsidies to its agricultural sector make it the most liberal among its trading partners. As a result of the prompt and visionary actions of the first elected governments in Estonia, the loss of trade with Estonia's former Soviet and other Eastern European countries was quickly rebuilt by intensifying its trading relations with Germany and Scandinavia.

In 1995 Estonia and the EU signed the Europe Agreement. It came into force at the beginning of 1998, after three years of lengthy negotiations (*see* Table 6.2).

Table 6.2 Evolution of the relationship between Estonia and the EU

Date	Stage of application	Additional comments
27 August 1991	The EU recognized Estonian independence	Diplomatic relations established between the EU and Estonia
November 1994	Estonia became an 'associated partner' to the EU	
1 January 1995	Free Trade Agreement with the EU concluded	Free Trade Agreement without a transition period was signed on 18 July 1994
12 June 1995	Europe Agreement (also known as the Association Agreement) signed	

Date	Stage of application	Additional comments
24 November 1995	Official application for EU membership submitted	
1 February 1998	The Europe Agreement came into force	It went through a lengthy ratification process
31 March 1998	Accession negotiations between the EU and Estonia began	
April 1998	Analytical examination of the *acquis* began	Concluded in autumn 1999
October 1998	The Commission issued its first Regular Report on Estonia	
November 1998	Membership negotiations began	
	Accession Partnership/National Programme for the Adoption of the *Acquis*	Outlines the strategy for accession
October 1999	The Commission issued its second Regular Report on Estonia	
February 2000	Update of the screening exercise began	Takes into account the new *acquis* that had been adopted in March 1998
November 2000	The Commission issued its third Regular Report on Estonia	

Sources: European Commission (2000) *Regular Report on Estonia's Progress Towards Accession*, November; Foreign Ministry of Estonia, Government of the Republic of Estonia, and European Commission Directorate-General for Economic and Financial Affairs (2000) *Joint Assessment of the Economic Policy Priorities of the Republic of Estonia*, Brussels, 28 March; European Commission, Economic and Social Committee (2000) *Estonia's Progress Towards Accession*, Brussels, 12 July.

MEETING EU REQUIREMENTS FOR ENTRY

Estonia has transformed its economic, political and social structure remarkably. Its bid for an early accession seems justified, since it has fulfilled the main criteria for entry:

- democratic institutions have been established;
- a functioning market economy with an extensively liberal trade regime is in place;
- economic incentives and an appropriate legal framework have helped people to adapt to reforms and engage in profit-maximizing businesses;
- a substantial amount of work on national legislation has been completed, in line with the EU book of laws, the *acquis communautaire*.

Meeting political criteria

Estonia meets the political criteria. However, there was some concern on the part of the EU when the minority non-Estonian speakers (Russian speakers) were barred from political and economic life. This issue has now been addressed, together with other issues such as:[3]

- the adoption of the State Integration Programme for non-Estonians;
- the reinforcement in the training of judges;
- the reduction in the number of judge vacancies;
- the improvement of the capacity of the Citizenship and Migration Board to handle residence and citizenship applications.

Some amendments in these areas have been introduced:

In its 1999 Regular Report on Estonia, the European Commission took a tough stance on Estonia's Language Law, which restricted access of non-Estonian speakers in political and economic life. In April 2000 Estonia introduced some necessary amendments to the law in order to comply with this requirement under the Europe Agreement.

A shortage of competent staff in public administration prevents various ministries and other government agencies from implementing a more extensive reform of the civil service and from executing a comprehensive administrative strategy.

The operation of the penal and civil law system requires more serious remedies. Judges still experience a great deal of pressure from a heavy workload. The backlog in the system is a big concern for Estonia. Court proceedings in the fight against crime still take a long time to complete – civil cases take on average in excess of four months.

Regarding minority rights, the programme for integrating non-Estonians into the country needs to be continued. Steps have been taken to improve the capacity of the Citizenship and Migration Board in order to handle residence and citizenship applications.

Meeting economic criteria

Estonia has been one of the most progressive of transition economies in Eastern Europe, even prior to its independence (1991) from Russia.

Estonia carried out small-scale privatization between 1991 and 1993. It began large-scale privatization in 1993, with most enterprises privatized by 1995. A widespread liberalization of market forces was pursued with a particular urgency and agility in order to secure a more rapid and comprehensive transition from the planned economy. What followed was an economic stabilization programme that had to be put in place to prevent the economy sliding towards hyperinflation.

Meeting obligations of membership

Estonia has provisionally closed 16 chapters of the *acquis communautaire* out of the 29 chapters that the country has opened. Table 6.3 shows the state of play of accession negotiations carried out with the EU.

Table 6.3 Estonia: state of negotiations on chapters of the *acquis communautaire* (at start of 2001)

Chapter	Title	State of play	Date
1	Free movement of goods	✓	Nov. 2000
2	Freedom of movement for persons	O	
3	Freedom to provide services	O	
4	Free movement of capital	✓	June 2000
5	Company law	✓	June 2000
6	Competition policy	O	
7	Agriculture	O	
8	Fisheries	✓	June 2000
9	Transport policy	O	
10	Taxation	O	
11	Economic and monetary union	✓	Dec. 1999
12	Statistics	✓	June 1999
13	Social policy and employment	✓	
14	Energy	O	
15	Industrial policy	✓	June 1999
16	Small and medium-sized undertakings	✓	Nov. 1998
17	Science and research	✓	Nov. 1998
18	Education and training	✓	Nov. 1998
19	Telecommunications and information technologies	✓	June 1999
20	Culture and audio-visual policy	✓	Nov. 2000
21	Regional policy and co-ordination of structural instruments	O	
22	Environment	O	
23	Consumers and health protection	✓	June 1999
24	Co-operation in the fields of justice and home affairs	O	
25	Customs union	O	

Chapter	Title	State of play	Date
26	External relations	✓	June 2000
27	Common foreign and security policy	✓	June 2000
28	Financial control	O	
29	Financial and budgetary provisions	O	
30	Institutions		
31	Other		
Total chapters opened		29	(Start of 2001)
Total chapters provisionally closed		16	(Start of 2001)

O = chapter opened, under negotiation; ✓ = chapter provisionally closed.

Source: European Commission (2000) Directorate-General Enlargement.

TIMING OF ACCESSION

With a small population of one and a half million, Estonia can hardly be a burden for the EU as a member. Given its efforts to reform and comply with the requirements of the EU, it is most likely that it will be included in the first round, whenever the first round may be. It is likely to be in the first round whether or not the EU takes on board a smaller group of countries, say in 2004 or 2005.

The level of public support in Estonia for joining the EU stands at around 60 per cent. Among the elite there is a larger level of support for EU membership and the commitment is to enter with the 'first wave' of accession, aiming for 2004.

Notes

1   Government of the Republic of Estonia and European Commission Directorate-General for Economic and Financial Affairs (2000) *Joint Assessment of the Economic Policy Priorities of the Republic of Estonia*, 28 March, Brussels, p. 4.

2   See Sepp, U., Vesilind, A. and Kaasik, U. (2000) 'Modelling inflation: an application to Estonia', *Economic and Financial Modelling*, (7) 3, Autumn.

3   European Commission (2000) *Regular Report on Estonia's Progress Towards Accession*, November, pp. 18 and 76.

Slovenia

OVERVIEW

Slovenia is one of the most eligible economies among the applicant countries in terms of compatibility with the EU. The country's per capita GDP is almost on a par with that of Portugal and Greece – two of the existing EU member countries. It is striking how far Slovenia's per capita income lies above that of the next highest income among the applicant countries – the Czech Republic. Slovenia's per capita income is almost 2500 euros above that of the latter.

Slovenia declared its independence in June 1991 and the EU officially recognized it as an independent state at the beginning of 1992. A significant feature of Slovenia is that it does not have a common border with Serbia and has been isolated from the latter's political upheaval and instabilities.

Table 7.1 provides an overview of the main economic indicators in Slovenia. Although Slovenia was originally an agricultural economy, over the past decades it has experienced a steady shift away from agriculture to industry. While this trend was intensified during the 1980s, before it broke away from the former Yugoslavia, it has still continued after its independence. By the mid-1990s the share of agriculture in GDP fell to a mere 5 per cent of gross domestic output, with employment in this sector absorbing only 5 per cent of the workforce.

Table 7.1 Overview of the Slovenian economy

Population average (millions)(1999)[1]	1.986
Gross Domestic Product(GDP)(per capita at current prices)(US$)(1999)[2]	10,992
GDP per capita (Purchasing Power Standards* in euros)(as of end 1999)[1]	14,964
GDP per capita (Purchasing Power Standards)(per cent of EU average)(1999)[1]	71
GDP at current prices (billion euros)(1999)[1]	18.7
Inflation rate, annual average (September 2000**)[1]	8.9
Appreciation/depreciation of national currency against the euro/Ecu (2001) (1997=100)[3]	83.06

Sources: [1] Eurostat (2000); [2] IMF (2000) *World Economic Outlook Database*, September; [3] Datastream.

Notes: * Eurostat defines Purchasing Power Standards as an artificial currency to enable correct comparison of volume of goods and services produced by different countries. Figures have been calculated using the population figures from National Accounts, which may differ from those used in demographic statistics.
** Moving 12-month average rate of change.

Industry in Slovenia primarily comprises:

- manufacture of basic metals
- metal products
- machinery and equipment
- chemicals

- electrical goods
- food and wooden products.

Exports act as the engine for economic growth. Domestic expenditure is essentially driven by the public sector demand. Private sector demand has been more restrained by the government control on wage rises.

PROCESS OF EU ACCESSION

Table 7.2 depicts the evolution of the relationship of Slovenia and the EU, including the stages of application and negotiations for EU membership by Slovenia.

Table 7.2 Evolution of the relationship between Slovenia and the EU

Date	Stage of application	Additional comments
January 1992	The EU recognized Slovenia's independence	Followed the declaration of independence
June 1996	Europe Agreement signed. Official application for EU membership submitted	
December 1997	The Luxembourg European Council recommended that accession negotiations begin[1]	
March 1998	Accession negotiations began	
April 1998	Analytical examination of the *acquis* began	
October 1998	The Commission issued its first Regular Report on Slovenia	
February 1999	Europe Agreement came into force	
October 1999	The Commission issued its second Regular Report on Slovenia	
Autumn 1999	Analytical examination of the *acquis* concluded[2]	
February 2000	Update of the examination of the *acquis* began	Takes into account the new *acquis* that had been adopted in March 1998
October 2000	The Commission issued its third Regular Report on Slovenia	

Sources: [1] European Council (1997) *Luxembourg European Council: Presidency Conclusions*, 12–13 December 1997; [2] European Commission (2000) *Regular Report on Slovenia's Progress Towards Accession*, November.

MEETING EU REQUIREMENTS FOR ENTRY

In the last decade of the twentieth century, Slovenia transformed itself from a socialist state into a modern democratic republic.

Meeting political criteria

Slovenia satisfies the Copenhagen political criteria and was accepted by the European Commission as a state with stable institutions that guarantee democracy, the rule of law, human rights and the accommodation of interests of minority groups. The Commission, however, has recommended further improvements be made in the judicial and parliamentary process.

In its recent past the functioning of democratic principles of political governance in Slovenia is visible and new parliamentary elections were held in October 2000 and the constitution is closely followed.

The European Commission has expressed concern at the country's unnecessarily slow legislative process. The system of three readings for every law, which ensures that all political factions in the Parliament have a chance to participate in the drafting process, delays the process of government reform. As the passing of the *acquis communautaire* dominates the agenda of the Parliament, it has introduced extraordinary sessions to accelerate the process. A proposal to change the current parliamentary procedure and the three-reading system failed to be implemented. This was because the requirement of the support of a two-thirds majority of the delegates could not be achieved.

During the year 2000 the Slovenian Parliament reached a decision to change the country's constitution. By this token it aims to conclude the debate on the present voting system, which had started, following a referendum in 1996 on the subject.

Further restructuring of the public administration system and an introduction of a civil service law is deemed of paramount importance. The creation of a fully-fledged civil service necessitates that three sets of laws are passed by Parliament and implemented. These are:

- the Law on Public Agencies;
- the Law on Government;
- the Law on Civil Servants.

With regard to the rule of law, there still remains a great deal to be done in speeding up court procedures. Some improvements have been witnessed in the year 2000. In order to speed up the processing of court cases the Government and the Supreme Court introduced two measures:

- efficiency-enhancement programmes and
- special financial incentives for increasing productivity in courts.

The new Law on Courts may also open new routes to deal with a growing number of unresolved court cases. By installing a system of 'rotating judges' it is hoped to assist district courts in coping with the workload. By giving the presidents of courts wider scope for self-organization, this amended law will ensure that they exert more will in *reducing the backlog of cases*.

In contrast to other Central European candidates, Slovenia's problem of corruption presents little cause for concern and appears to be on a limited scale. In accordance with the 1999 legal framework for anti-corruption measures, a new anti-corruption measure within the police was created. Moreover, a new 'Organised Crime Section' in the Ministry of the Interior and a group of public prosecutors for special assignments were established.

Meeting economic criteria

Slovenia is close to fulfilling the economic requirements stipulated by the European Council in Copenhagen in June 1993.[1] The fiscal and the external balances are under control, providing the basis for macroeconomic stability. However, there are some areas that still require further action:

- There is macroeconomic instability in terms of prices and public finance. Inflation has been accelerating, due to higher oil prices and the indexing of wages and pensions. The weak currency is another source of instability. The Central Bank of Slovenia needs to adjust its monetary policy. Long-term reforms are called for in order to sustain the increasing costs of the pension system and the dismissing of workers.

- There is a lack of competition within the financial market. The reorganization of the banking and insurance sector has been slow. There are still many restrictions on short-term capital movements.

- The market in Slovenia does not function completely freely, in that the state still controls many sectors and the agricultural policy is very protectionist. The role of the Government should be reduced and competition should be encouraged. Prices of energy and basic food, such as milk, are far from being liberalized. Restrictions still exist on foreign investment. It is quite difficult to obtain business permits, given the high level of bureaucracy in the legal system.

- There are barriers to market exit. The procedures of bankruptcy are very slow, which in turn makes market exit difficult. The system is reluctant to allow bankruptcy to materialize; usually loss-making companies are re-organized or re-capitalized and so prevented from closing down.

Meeting obligations of membership

Slovenia has provisionally closed 14 chapters of the *acquis communautaire* out of the 29 chapters that it opened (*see* Table 7.3).

Table 7.3 Slovenia: state of negotiations on chapters of the *acquis communautaire* (at start of 2001)

Chapter	Title	State of play	Date
1	Free movement of goods	O	
2	Freedom of movement for persons	O	
3	Freedom to provide services	✓	Nov. 2000
4	Free movement of capital	O	
5	Company law	✓	June 2000
6	Competition policy	O	
7	Agriculture	O	
8	Fisheries	✓	June 1999
9	Transport policy	O	
10	Taxation	O	
11	Economic and monetary union	✓	Dec. 1999
12	Statistics	✓	June 1999
13	Social policy and employment	✓	Nov. 2000
14	Energy	[✓]	
15	Industrial policy	✓	June 1999
16	Small and medium-sized undertakings	✓	Nov. 1998
17	Science and research	✓	Nov. 1998
18	Education and training	✓	Nov. 1998
19	Telecommunications and information technologies	✓	June 1999
20	Culture and audio-visual policy	O	
21	Regional policy and co-ordination of structural instruments	O	
22	Environment	O	
23	Consumers and health protection	✓	June 1999
24	Co-operation in the fields of justice and home affairs	O	
25	Customs union	O	
26	External relations	O	
27	Common foreign and security policy	✓	June 2000
28	Financial control	✓	June 2000
29	Financial and budgetary provisions	O	
30	Institutions		
31	Other		
Total chapters opened		29	(Start of 2001)
Total chapters provisionally closed		14	(Start of 2001)

O = chapter opened, under negotiation; ✓ = chapter provisionally closed; [✓] = chapter for which the Commission has proposed provisional closure.

Source: European Commission (2000) Directorate-General Enlargement.

TIMING OF ACCESSION

Slovenia has an economy that, among the applicant countries, most closely resembles that of the EU members and perhaps could most readily become united with the rest of the EU. If it were politically feasible, Slovenia could be admitted almost immediately. However, ultimately the decision of the EU on enlargement will not be based on technical grounds but rather on political considerations. Therefore, the decision as to when to admit Slovenia will rest upon when some of the other front-runners are ready. In particular, it will depend upon when Poland is ready – or rather upon when the EU decides it is time to go ahead with enlargement. An enlargement without Poland is considered inconceivable.

The results of our study show that Slovenia should be in the first round of accession whenever the EU expansion takes place. If the first round is scheduled for 2005, then that will be Slovenia's timing of accession.

Note

1 European Commission (2000) *Regular Report on Slovenia's Progress Towards Accession*, November, pp. 20–28.

8

Cyprus

OVERVIEW

Cyprus has had a long-standing relationship with the EU dating back to 1972. The evolution of the relationship of the country with the European Union is shown in Table 8.2. From a purely economic viewpoint, among all the 13 applicant countries, the islands of Malta and Cyprus (*see* Table 8.1) seem to be the 'best equipped' to join the EU. In fact, in one of the scenarios envisaged in the EU expansion debates and discussions, Cyprus and Malta are considered to be the first two applicant countries that could be admitted to the EU. That is, the enlargement of the EU could commence with admitting just these two countries. However, there are many other scenarios for the variety of forms that the EU expansion could take which are discussed in Chapter 1.

Table 8.1 Overview of the economy of Cyprus

Population average (millions)(at the end of the year 1999)[1]	0.667
Gross Domestic Product(GDP)(per capita at current prices)(US$)(1999)[2]	13,962
GDP per capita (Purchasing Power Standards* in euros)(as of end 1999)[1]	17,082
GDP per capita (Purchasing Power Standards*)(per cent of EU average)(1999)[1]	81
GDP at current prices (billion euros)(1999)[1]	8.5
Inflation rate, annual average (June 2000**)[1]	3.4
Appreciation/depreciation of national currency against the euro/Ecu (2001) (1997=100)[3]	102.602

Sources: [1] Eurostat (2000); [2] IMF (2000) *World Economic Outlook Database*, September; [3] Datastream.

Notes: * Eurostat defines Purchasing Power Standards as an artificial currency to enable correct comparison of volume of goods and services produced by different countries. Figures have been calculated using the population figures from National Accounts, which may differ from those used in demographic statistics. ** Moving 12-month average rate of change.

PROCESS OF EU ACCESSION

The relationship between Cyprus and the EU (at that time known as the EEC) can be traced back to the early 1970s. Table 8.2 provides an overview of the development of the EU relationship with Cyprus.

The Europe Agreement with the EU was signed in 1972, to set up a customs union that was to be implemented in two stages.[1] Stage 1 involved a phased reduction of tariffs on agricultural and industrial goods. Stage 2 involved final fulfilment of all aspects of a customs union. This latter was in turn split into two separate stages. The customs union is to be finally completed in 2002 or 2003.

| Table 8.2 | Evolution of the relationship between Cyprus and the EU |

Date	Stage of application	Additional comments
December 1972	Association Agreement (also known as Europe Agreement) was signed[2]	The Association Agreement was designed for a customs union and implemented in two stages
June 1973	Association Agreement signed in 1972 came into force	
1987	Customs Union Protocol established	
Late 1987	The aims of the first stage of the Association Agreement (originally scheduled for completion 1977 later extended to 1987) were achieved[1]	Included the phased reduction of tariffs on industrial goods and agricultural products
1 January 1988	Protocol for first phase of the second stage of the Association Agreement enforced	Involved reduction of customs duties, and adoption of the EU's Common Customs Tariff
4 July 1990	Cyprus submitted its application for accession to the EU	
1993	EU Commission on Cyprus issued a positive Opinion on Cyprus's application	
June 1994	The European Council confirmed that the next round of the EU's enlargement would involve Cyprus (and Malta)	
12 June 1995	The EU/Cyprus Association Council adopted a common resolution on the establishment of a structured dialogue between the EU and Cyprus and on certain elements of the strategy to prepare it for accession	
1997	First phase of the second stage of the Agreement achieved	
1997	Second phase of the second stage of the agreement enforced	Due to be completed by 2002
January 1998	First phase of EC–Cyprus Customs Union completed	
October 1998	The Commission issued its first Regular Report on Cyprus	

Date	Stage of application	Additional comments
31 March 1998	Accession negotiations between the EU and Cyprus were launched	Followed the go-ahead given at the Luxembourg Summit
October 1999	The Commission issued its second Regular Report on Cyprus	
March 2000	Accession Partnership was established by a Council Decision	
October 2000	The Commission issued its third Regular Report on Cyprus	

Sources: [1] European Commission (2000) *Regular Report on Cyprus's Progress Towards Accession*, November; Delegation of the European Commission to Cyprus (2000) European Economic and Financial Centre, *Cyprus – European Union: a Brief History;* Cyprus Government *Cyprus and EU Accession Negotiations.*

The accession negotiations formally commenced in March 1998, following the go-ahead given by the Luxembourg European Council in December 1997.

MEETING EU REQUIREMENTS FOR ENTRY

One of the most significant problems holding back Cyprus from accession has been the conflict between the Turkish Cypriots and the Greek Cypriots. The hostilities between the groups caused the division of the island between the two factions. For a better understanding of this conflict, a brief history of Cyprus may provide some enlightenment.

Cyprus remained under Turkish domination until 1878, when, with the Treaty of Berlin, the Sultan of Turkey left Cyprus to Great Britain, in order to obtain British aid in the war against the Russians.[2]

In 1925 Cyprus became a British colony. In August 1960 Cyprus obtained its independence from the UK with an agreement among Greece, Turkey and the UK that guaranteed the Greek and Turkish cohabitation under the presidency of Archbishop Makarios. In the same year Cyprus became a member of the United Nations, the Commonwealth and, in 1961, of the Council of Europe (a consultative assembly formed in 1949).

The Greek coup of 15 July 1974, supported by Athens, tried to annex Cyprus to Greece, so provoking the reaction of Turkey. The north-eastern part of the island was occupied by Turkish troops, who founded an independent state (in 1975) that, in 1983, assumed the name of the 'Turkish Republic of Cyprus of the North'. No other country of the world apart from Turkey has recognized the status of this state. The island then remained divided as two national entities: the Greek side to the south, which claims the sovereignty on all the territory, and the Turkish side to the north, which stands alone and claims an independent status.

From 1985, the United Nations has been trying unsuccessful mediations in order to overcome the political division of the island.

Meeting political criteria

Cyprus 'continues to meet' the political criteria as part of the 1993 Copenhagen Criteria.[3]

The island's two communities have been working closely as partners, as stipulated in the Accession Partnership. During the period 1999–2000 there has been some slight progress with discussions aimed at finding a solution. It was evident in the fourth series of meetings held between the EU and Cyprus that there may be hopes of a breakthrough. The proximity talks that took place in September 2000 indicated that the two opposing regions of the country are negotiating with each other.

Meeting economic criteria

Cyprus satisfies the two principle requirements of the economic criteria. The country is considered by the European Commission as having a 'functioning market economy' as well as being equipped to 'cope with competitive pressures and market forces in the Union'.

Meeting obligations of membership

The Luxembourg European Council in December 1997 recommended that the formal accession negotiations should commence with Cyprus in 1998.

The 'analytical' verification of the *acquis communautaire* for an applicant country is referred to as the process of 'screening'. This exercise was carried out for Cyprus by the European Commission over the period Spring to Autumn 1998.

Since the start of accession negotiations in March 1998 Cyprus has taken part in four rounds of ministerial negotiations. These were held under the different rotating presidencies of the EU. France held the Presidency during July–December 2000; Portugal: January–June 2000; Finland: July–December 1999; and Germany: January–June 1999. Seventeen chapters of the *acquis* have been provisionally closed (*see* Table 8.3).

The 17 chapters of the *acquis* that have been provisionally closed are: Company Law; Fisheries; Transport Policy; Economic and Monetary Union; Statistics; Employment and Social Affairs; Industrial Policy; Small and Medium Sized Undertakings; Science and Research; Education and Training; Telecommunication and Information Technologies; Culture and Audio-Visual Policy; Consumer and Health Protection; Customs Union; External Relations; Common Foreign and Security Policy as well as Financial Control.

Table 8.3 Cyprus: state of negotiations on chapters of the *acquis communautaire* (at start of 2001)

Chapter	Title	State of play	Date
1	Free movement of goods	✓	Nov. 2000
2	Freedom of movement for persons	O	
3	Freedom to provide services	O	
4	Free movement of capital	O	
5	Company law	✓	June 2000
6	Competition policy	O	
7	Agriculture	O	
8	Fisheries	✓	June 2000
9	Transport policy	[✓]	
10	Taxation	O	
11	Economic and monetary union	✓	Dec. 1999
12	Statistics	✓	June 1999
13	Social policy and employment	✓	June 2000
14	Energy	O	
15	Industrial policy	✓	Nov. 1998
16	Small and medium-sized undertakings	✓	Nov. 1998
17	Science and research	✓	Nov. 1998
18	Education and training	✓	Nov. 1998
19	Telecommunications and information technologies	✓	June 1999
20	Culture and audio-visual policy	✓	Nov. 1998
21	Regional policy and co-ordination of structural instruments	O	
22	Environment	O	
23	Consumers and health protection	✓	June 1999
24	Co-operation in the fields of justice and home affairs	O	
25	Customs union	✓	June 1999
26	External relations	✓	June 1999
27	Common foreign and security policy	✓	June 2000
28	Financial control	✓	June 2000
29	Financial and budgetary provisions	O	
30	Institutions		
31	Other		
Total chapters opened		29	(Start of 2001)
Total chapters provisionally closed		17	(Start of 2001)

O = chapter opened, under negotiation; ✓ = chapter provisionally closed; [✓] = chapter for which the Commission has proposed provisional closure.

Source: European Commission (2000) Directorate-General Enlargement.

TIMING OF ACCESSION

Cyprus has completed 17 of the 29 chapters opened. Accordingly, among the 13 applicant countries, it has the highest number of the 'provisionally closed' chapters. The main stumbling block has been the splitting of the island between the Turkish-speaking and Greek-speaking parts. If this issue is resolved, Cyprus could be among the front-runners, for it has a market economy. Its GDP per capita is around 80 per cent of the EU average per capita, as Table 8.1 shows. Indeed, the country has the ingredients of an eligible member.

If the political problem with respect to the division of the island is resolved in time, Cyprus could be included in the first round of new members if the first wave happens in 2004/2005. In the absence of a breakthrough in discussions with Turkish Cyprus, the country could be put back in the waiting room until the matter is resolved.

Notes

1   Delegation of the European Commission to Cyprus (2000).

2   Marco Sassano (1998) *Piccolo Atlante dei Sei Paesi*, Dossier Europa, June, n. 22 pp. 48–49.

3   European Commission (2000) *Regular Report on Cyprus' Progress Towards Accession*, November.

Malta

9

OVERVIEW

Malta possesses the essential ingredients of an 'open' trading economy and is a member of the World Trade Organization (WTO). The economy is sufficiently developed and as such the country will have to relinquish its ranking as a 'developing country' when it enters the EU.[1] The Maltese economy can be described as an open economy,[2] with exports featuring 50 per cent of value-added and the size of imports equalling that of GDP. Table 9.1 provides some insights into the structure of the economy.

Table 9.1 Overview of the Maltese economy

Population average (millions)(1999)[1]	0.388
Gross Domestic Product(GDP)(per capita at current prices)(US$)(1999)[2]	10,424
GDP per capita (Purchasing Power Standards* in euros)(as of end 1999)[1]	–
GDP per capita (Purchasing Power Standards)(per cent of EU average)(1999)[1]	–
GDP at current prices (billion euros)(1999)[1]	3.4
Inflation rate, annual average (January–August 2000**)[1]	2.6
Appreciation/depreciation of national currency against the euro/Ecu (2001) (1997=100)[3]	110.23

Sources: [1] Eurostat (2000); [2] IMF (2000) *World Economic Outlook Database*, September; [3] Datastream.

Notes: * Eurostat defines Purchasing Power Standards as an artificial currency to enable correct comparison of volume of goods and services produced by different countries. Figures have been calculated using the population figures from National Accounts, which may differ from those used in demographic statistics.
** Moving 12-month average rate of change.

Malta lacks any significant natural resources and as such the economy relies heavily on tourism and assembling activities (i.e. mounting components together), which in turn rely on foreign resources. Electronics are replacing textiles as the significant manufacturing industry. Production is quite varied, despite a workforce of only 140,000.

PROCESS OF EU ACCESSION

Malta submitted its application for membership of the EU in two stages. First the Maltese Government, held by the National Party, applied in 1990. However, the Malta Labour Party (MLP) won the general election of October 1996 and halted the Maltese application for EU membership in 1996. The National Party re-applied in September 1998, following its return to power after the general election (*see* Table 9.2).

Table 9.2 Evolution of the relationship between Malta and the EU

Date	Stages of application	Additional comments
16 July 1990	The Maltese Government submitted its application for EU membership[1]	
June 1993	The Commission submitted its 'Opinion' on Malta to the Council[1]	
October 1996	Application for EU membership put on hold[1]	The application was frozen by the newly elected government (Malta Labour Party) (1)
September 1998	Application for EU membership re-initiated[1]	The application was re-initiated following the re-election of the National Party in the general elections (1)
5 October 1998	The Council invited the Commission to 'present an update of the 1993 Opinion on Malta's application for membership in the EU'[1]	
17 February 1999	The Commission submitted its Opinion on Malta's application for membership in the EU[1]	
October 1999	The Commission issued its 1999 Regular Report on Malta	
12 December 1999	EU member states endorsed accession negotiations with Malta at Helsinki Summit	Following a recommendation by the Commission on 13 October 1999
February 2000	Negotiations were officially opened at a bilateral intergovernmental conference[2]	Negotiations commenced on eight chapters of the *acquis* (2); a further nine chapters were opened later in 2000
November 2000	The Commission issued its 2000 Regular Report on Malta	

Sources: [1] European Commission (1999) *Regular Report from the Commission on Malta's Progress Towards Accession*; [2] European Commission (2000) *Regular Report on Malta's Progress Towards Accession*, November.

Following this second application, on 5 October 1998 the European Council asked the Commission to prepare a new 'Opinion' based on the report they prepared on the previous application of the country. More specifically, this report was to follow and bring up to date the previous Commission's Opinion, put forward to the Council in June 1993, which was prepared after Malta's first application for the Community membership (in July 1990).[3] For the purpose of this updated report, the European Commission collected information on the conditions of Malta, through cooperation between EU experts and Maltese authorities.

In March 1999 Malta was asked by the European Commission to state its National Programme for the Adoption of the *Acquis* (NPAA), as instructed by the General Affairs Council. Subsequently in May 1999, the so-called 'screening' process, which is the initial phase of the negotiations, began with nine chapters of the *acquis*.[4]

MEETING EU REQUIREMENTS FOR ENTRY

This section analyses the three main requirements of entry: the political criteria, the economic criteria, and obligations of membership for Malta.

Meeting political criteria

Malta fulfils the Copenhagen political criteria (as explained in Chapter 1). However, there remain certain areas that are of concern with respect to EU accession:

- The functioning of the 'executive' has to be improved. To comply with the Accession Partnership it is necessary to establish a more streamlined and better-organized public administration system. The Government has made certain strides in this respect but it is too early to evaluate their success.

- The judiciary system has to operate more efficiently. Although the actual structure of the judiciary is satisfactory (and the judiciary is autonomous from the executive), proceedings are sluggish. Between 1995 and the end of 2000 the backlog of cases has risen, indicating that Malta may be incapable of actually enforcing the European Convention of Human Rights (adopted into Malta's constitution), which demands that just action is taken within an acceptable timescale. Attempts to resolve this situation (for example, establishing the Commission for Administration) have not demonstrated any success in late 2000.

- The problem of corruption has not been fully addressed and the required anti-corruption measures have not been introduced.

- Malta needs to upgrade its capacity to cope with asylum seekers (despite progress made in 2000). This has to include an effort to assimilate approved refugees into Maltese society, acceptable housing for the refugees, the infrastructure to cope with refugees, and an improvement on the method of rejection.

Meeting economic criteria

On the whole Malta has maintained inflation at a low level. At the start of 2000 the general level of prices began to rise in response to the following variables:

- growing public demand;
- the addition of VAT on goods derived from oil and on telephone facilities;
- lower subsidies on bread and bus fares.

Not all prices are liberalized, particularly of basic commodities and domestic manufactured goods. For political and social reasons the Government determines prices in many public entities (for example, Water Services Corporation and Enemalta). Enemalta (supplying energy) risks falling into the red, as prices do not reflect rising petroleum costs.

The Government is required to reduce its influential role in Malta's economy. For a more competitive economic climate, the Government has to continue its privatization, lower the government subsidies, and has to create a more liberal trade and capital system.

Although the shortfall in public finances is somewhat declining, the budget deficit is still of concern. Despite the fact that the government has had to cope with rising remuneration in the public sector and the removal of some subsidies, there is a need to cut public spending further to a sustainable level in the longer run. The Commission on Welfare Reform holds the responsibility for reorganizing the social benefits scheme, but little action has been taken so far.

Despite progress between 1997 and 1999, the external account deteriorated in 2000. The volume of imports rose to satisfy the demands of the electronic, paper and automobile sectors. Rising oil costs and the decline in the number of tourists also had a negative impact. The Government can meet the shortfall only through privatization revenues and funds raised from international banks, since government debt rose by 4 per cent of GDP to a total of 60 per cent of Gross Domestic Product in 2000.

Meeting obligations of membership

In the space of one year Malta has been able to close 12 chapters of the *acquis communautaire* out of the 17 chapters that it opened. This is quite commendable considering some countries that began their accession negotiations in 1998 managed to close only 13 chapters (the Czech Republic and Poland) or 14 chapters (Slovenia and Hungary). Of course, these countries have much higher populations and they inherited their economies from the former communist regimes and therefore had to substantially liberalize – problems that Malta does not have to face.

There remain 12 more chapters to be opened in the course of 2001 (*see* Table 9.3).

Table 9.3 Malta: state of negotiations on chapters of the *acquis communautaire* (at start of 2001)

Chapter	Title	State of play	Date
1	Free movement of goods	~	
2	Freedom of movement for persons	~	
3	Freedom to provide services	~	
4	Free movement of capital	O	
5	Company law	✓	Nov. 2000
6	Competition policy	O	
7	Agriculture	~	
8	Fisheries	O	
9	Transport policy	O	
10	Taxation	~	
11	Economic and monetary union	✓	Nov. 2000
12	Statistics	✓	Nov. 2000
13	Social policy and employment	O	
14	Energy	~	
15	Industrial policy	✓	May 2000
16	Small and medium-sized undertakings	✓	May 2000
17	Science and research	✓	May 2000
18	Education and training	✓	May 2000
19	Telecommunications and information technologies	✓	May 2000
20	Culture and audio-visual policy	✓	Nov. 2000
21	Regional policy and co-ordination of structural instruments	~	
22	Environment	~	
23	Consumers and health protection	✓	Nov. 2000
24	Co-operation in the fields of justice and home affairs	~	
25	Customs union	~	
26	External relations	✓	May 2000
27	Common foreign and security policy	✓	May 2000
28	Financial control	~	
29	Financial and budgetary provisions	~	
30	Institutions		
31	Other		
Total chapters opened		17	(Start of 2001)
Total chapters provisionally closed		12	(Start of 2001)

O = chapter opened, under negotiation; ✓ = chapter provisionally closed; ~ = chapter not yet opened to negotiation.

Source: European Commission (2000) Directorate-General Enlargement.

TIMING OF ACCESSION

Malta does not expect to enter the EU before 2005. That is, Malta would be satisfied if it were allowed membership in 2005. However, negotiating parties in the Maltese government acknowledge that the process could take longer (possibly until 2006).

Malta qualifies as one of the front-runners in the enlargement process. Although it may be ambitious to group Malta alongside the likes of Hungary, Estonia and Slovenia, this small state is certainly closely behind them, having fulfilled the necessary political and economic requirements. However, as with all candidate countries, there remain areas of concern to be addressed within political and economic spheres. While there are no quantitative guidelines to assess each 'area of concern', it is nevertheless fair to say that they should not pose significant obstacles to accession.

The Government has taken a realistic stance on the public finance situation through a six-year plan that is expected to bring the structural deficit to a sustainable level of 3–4 per cent of GDP by 2004[5] from 8.6 per cent of GDP in 1999. The Commission identifies the role of the Government in the economy as a problem, particularly its role in controlling prices. While this needs to be addressed it is important to note that with some of the existing member states there also exist controlled prices. Thus it is possible to conclude that the essential conditions within the Copenhagen Criteria have been fulfilled and that Malta presents a good case for accession.

Politically Malta also fulfils the Copenhagen Criteria, demonstrating democracy in its institutions. Although the judiciary is slow, it is structurally adequate. The speed of the judiciary may prove to be a downfall if efforts to improve the situation do not take effect soon. There is also the anxiety that it may fail to enforce the European Convention on Human Rights. Corruption continues to tarnish Malta's reputation, although it is not possible to quantify its impact on the country's progress towards accession.

In short, the above-mentioned lack of conformity with the EU should not pose significant obstacles to Malta's accession. When Malta has closed all of the *acquis* chapters it will be in a position to join the EU (barring any deterioration in economic and political proceedings).

It would be no surprise if Malta were to be included among the first to join the EU, since the country has been preparing since 1990, despite withdrawing its application in the mid 1990s. An extra boost to Malta's campaign for entry may be reached during the Spanish Presidency, as Spain would prefer a stronger Mediterranean presence in the EU. Malta's small size only acts to heighten the country's accession chances. This is because it is unlikely to impose a heavy financial burden on the existing member states, and its low population makes the feared mass outflow of labour improbable.

Notes

1   European Commission (1999) *Commission Opinion on Malta's Application for Membership of the European Union*, 17 February.

2   G. Cordina (1998) 'A structural econometric model of the Maltese economy', *Economic and Financial Modelling*, (5) 3, Autumn.

3   The European Commission (1999) *Regular Report on Malta's Progress Towards Accession*, October.

4   Ibid.

5   Maltese Ministry of Foreign Affairs (2000) *Malta National Programme for the Adoption of the Acquis*, 1 September.

Slovakia

OVERVIEW

Slovakia's accession negotiation for entry into the EU was approved in December 1999 and the actual negotiations commenced from February 2000. Yet in the space of a year the country managed to close ten chapters of the *acquis communautaire* as part of the requirement for entry. This is impressive and puts Slovakia ahead of some of the other applicant countries whose accession negotiations were approved at the same time.

During the Portuguese presidency (spanning January–June 2000) Slovakia opened eight *acquis* chapters and closed six. During the French presidency (July–December 2000) the country opened eight chapters and closed four. Thus, out of the 16 chapters that were opened during the year 2000 there remain only six still to be negotiated. In addition, Slovakia wishes to open 13 new chapters during the Swedish presidency (January–June 2001). Furthermore, Slovakia hopes to close all its accession negotiations on all the outstanding 19 chapters by the end of the Belgian presidency (July–December 2001).

Table 10.1 provides some insights into the structure of the Slovak economy.

Table 10.1 Overview of the Slovak economy

Population average (millions)(1999)[1]	5.395
Gross Domestic Product(GDP)(per capita at current prices)(US$)(1999)[2]	3,499
GDP per capita (Purchasing Power Standards* in euros)(as of end 1999)[1]	10,279
GDP per capita (Purchasing Power Standards)(per cent of EU average)(1999)[1]	49
GDP at current prices (billion euros)(1999)[1]	18.5
Inflation rate, annual average (September 2000**)[1]	13.6
Appreciation/depreciation of national currency against the euro/Ecu (2001) (1997=100)[3]	90.99

Sources: [1] Eurostat (2000); [2] IMF (2000) *World Economic Outlook Database*, September; [3] Datastream.

Notes: * Eurostat defines Purchasing Power Standards as an artificial currency to enable correct comparison of volume of goods and services produced by different countries. Figures have been calculated using the population figures from National Accounts, which may differ from those used in demographic statistics.
** Moving 12-month average rate of change.

PROCESS OF EU ACCESSION

Slovakia signed up to the Europe Agreement with the EU in October 1993 (*see* Table 10.2). Slovakia's official application for EU membership was not made until June 1995. Nevertheless, formal negotiations on Slovakian accession to the EU were given the green light by the European Commission in its 13 October 1999 Composite Paper,[1] which recommended that accession negotiations should commence.

Table 10.2 Evolution of the relationship between Slovakia and the EU

Date	Stage of application	Additional comments
October 1993	Europe Agreement signed	The Europe Agreement is a bilateral trade agreement between the EEC and Slovakia
February 1995	Europe Agreement came into force	
June 1995	Submitted its application for EU membership	
July 1995	EU Council of Ministers decided to implement consultation on membership	
November 1998	First submission by the European Commission of its Opinion on Slovakia to the European Council	
March 1998	Accession Partnership	Accession Partnership sets out the short and medium-term strategies and priorities as they pertain to the *acquis*
December 1999	EU member states endorsed the start of accession negotiations with Slovakia at Helsinki Summit	
15 February 2000	Opening of ministerial-level meetings of the Intergovernmental Conference (IGC) on Slovak accession to the EU[1]	
March 2000	First deputy-level meeting of the IGC in Brussels[1]	
May 2000	Second deputy-level meeting of the IGC in Brussels[1]	
June 2000	Second ministerial-level meeting of the IGC at Luxembourg[1]	

Sources: Slovakian Ministry of Foreign Affairs;
European Commission (2000).

The urgency for the Slovak Republic to be included in the first wave of new EU entrants intensified following the September 1998 election defeat of Meciar's administration. The incumbent government sought to fulfil the requirements of EU accession by adopting policies geared towards the promotion of competitiveness through reform of the enterprise sector. Specific attention was paid to the energy-intensive industrial manufacturing and the financial sectors, which included privatization of three major banks and an insurance company. The recovery of bad debt and the creation of a bank-restructuring agency was put on the agenda of reform for preparation to join the EU.

The 1999 Accession Partnership for Slovakia, published by the European Commission's Directorate-General on the Enlargement of the EU, specified the areas of improvement needed in Slovakia's domestic policy for alignment with the existing members of the EU.

In relation to border control policy towards Belarus, Russia and the Ukraine, since the monitoring of frontiers is still somewhat unsecured. The number of undocumented immigrants rose between 1998 and the autumn of 1999. This results from a lack of trained and equipped immigration officials. However, during the year 2000 Slovakia introduced visa stickers as a measure of control.

The Slovakian banking sector is visibly divided between banks that are owned by the public sector and those that are in the hands of the commercial sector. Of these two segments, each comprises roughly 50 per cent of the market. The smaller-sized banks are in the hands of the private sector, with heavy injection of foreign capital. They are making inroads into the Slovak financial sector and are taking away market share from the large banks operated by the public sector. The large state-owned banks require intensive overhaul and are in need of fresh capital.

Moreover, the substantial volume of bad debts has led to large spreads between the borrowing and lending rates of interest. This, in turn, poses a constraint for the development of the private sector – in particular for the small and medium-sized enterprises. However, the state-owned banks have been undergoing privatization and management restructuring, so making them more efficient.

MEETING EU REQUIREMENTS FOR ENTRY

Meeting political criteria

Slovakia continues to meet the political criteria laid down by the Copenhagen European Council in June 1993.[2] However, there are some areas that need to be addressed:

The weak functioning of Parliament and the civil service constitutes a major stumbling block. The refusal of the leading opposition to occupy posts in the parliamentary committees and supervisory bodies has delayed the legislative process. The result is that, in order to apply the *acquis communautaire*, the Parliament has to adopt 231 laws by 2002.

The legal system is still not functioning adequately and has to be improved. Judicial proceedings last an average of 12 months and the number of cases before the courts has tripled since the early 1990s.

Corruption is rampant and prevails across the board in Slovakia. Cases of corruption have been detected in the areas of health care, the labour office and the police, etc. Anti-corruption measures are rather general and lack organization. The system needs a more detailed plan of action.

In terms of civil and political rights, Slovakia made important improvements. However, there are some obstacles to a real freedom of expression. The state-owned television is still not giving a sufficient and objective coverage.

Further action is also needed in the fight against the trafficking in women. There is also a lack of legislation in terms of children and women's protection. Nearly 6000 abandoned children are living in inadequate conditions.

Little progress has been made in the area of implementation of laws in support of minority rights and the protection of minorities. Hardly any improvement is observed in the lives of minorities. The new plan for tackling the problem of the Roma community, adopted in September 1999, lacks definition of objectives and clarity in financial allocation or assessment of processes. The Roma minority in Slovakia continues to suffer discrimination and lack of police protection. The uncontrolled outflow of Slovaks of Romany origin to EU member countries has led to the imposition of visa requirements by Denmark, Belgium, Ireland and the UK on all Slovak citizens. This constitutes a big obstacle to the accession process.

Meeting economic criteria

Slovakia is close to meeting the economic requirements stipulated by the European Council in Copenhagen in June 1993.[3] However, there are some critical obstacles that need to be overcome:

The level of administered prices is still high (19.3 per cent of the consumer price index). The consequence of this is an acceleration of inflation.

Even though there are no more barriers to market entry, few new firms have been established. The new bankruptcy system should proceed faster and be implemented by a responsible court.

While the legal system is nominally in place and property rights are guaranteed, the level of corruption remains too high. The operation and functioning of the courts of law have to be improved for the enactment of business laws.

The medium-term sustainability of public finances is not yet ensured, which in turn could lead to macroeconomic instability in terms of public finance. Medium-term measures should concentrate on containing expenditures. The strategy of the public sector has to be geared towards reducing government expenditure and balancing the fiscal budget.

The financial sector is not sufficiently developed. Financial intermediation is high but the financial sector is suffering from the past conduct of the state-owned banks. Capital markets need to be restructured, since they are still fragmented and illiquid.

Despite the political disagreements within the ruling coalition, the Slovak Government has still succeeded in securing a broad consensus on economic policy.

Meeting obligations of membership

Slovakia has satisfied ten chapters of the *acquis communautaire* (*see* Table 10.3). This puts it ahead of some of the other four countries in the group of five who commenced negotiations in 2000. Among the other fellow entry countries, Latvia has satisfied nine chapters, Lithuania seven and Romania six.

Table 10.3 Slovakia: state of negotiations on chapters of the *acquis communautaire* (at start of 2001)

Chapter	Title	State of play	Date
1	Free movement of goods	~	
2	Freedom of movement for persons	~	
3	Freedom to provide services	O	
4	Free movement of capital	O	
5	Company law	~	
6	Competition policy	O	
7	Agriculture	~	
8	Fisheries	✓	Oct. 2000
9	Transport policy	O	
10	Taxation	~	
11	Economic and monetary union	~	
12	Statistics	✓	May 2000
13	Social policy and employment	~	
14	Energy	~	
15	Industrial policy	✓	Oct. 2000
16	Small and medium-sized undertakings	✓	May 2000
17	Science and research	✓	May 2000
18	Education and training	✓	May 2000
19	Telecommunications and information technologies	O	
20	Culture and audio-visual policy	✓	Nov. 2000
21	Regional policy and co-ordination of structural instruments	~	
22	Environment	~	

Chapter	Title	State of play	Date
23	Consumers and health protection	✓	Oct. 2000
24	Co-operation in the fields of justice and home affairs	~	
25	Customs union	O	
26	External relations	✓	May 2000
27	Common foreign and security policy	✓	May 2000
28	Financial control	~	
29	Financial and budgetary provisions	~	
30	Institutions		
31	Other		
Total chapters opened		16	(Start of 2001)
Total chapters provisionally closed		10	(Start of 2001)

O = chapter opened, under negotiation; ✓ = chapter provisionally closed; ~ = chapter not yet opened to negotiation.

Source: European Commission (2000) Directorate-General Enlargement.

TIMING OF ACCESSION

While the customs union between Slovakia and the Czech Republic could work against the latter, hindering its accession to the EU, it could work to the advantage of Slovakia, pushing it forward. That is, if all the preparations of Slovakia and the negotiations progress well.

Since Slovakia has made good progress with closing the chapters of the *acquis*, there is a very small chance that it could be included in the first round of entry, possibly in 2005.

Notes

1 European Commission (1999) *Composite Paper on the Commission Regular Reports 1999*, 13 October. The Composite Paper is drawn as a composition of the numerous European Commission Regular Reports on candidate countries since its initial submission to the European Council in November 1998 (COM[1999] 500-513 19/10).

2 European Commission (2000) *Regular Report on Slovakia's Progress Towards Accession*, November.

3 Ibid., pp. 23–32.

Latvia

OVERVIEW

Latvia considers its EU application for membership very seriously and has taken up itself to formulate a specific plan for preparing the country for entry into the EU. Accordingly, in the year 2000 the Government of Latvia published its *Strategy for Integration into the European Union*, setting out its tactics and procedures to achieve its accession to the EU.

Latvia is a small economy with a population of roughly two and a half million. Its per capita GDP is about a quarter of that of the EU per capita average. Table 11.1 presents the basic economic statistics for Latvia.

Table 11.1 Overview of the Latvian economy

Population average (millions)(1999)[1]	2.432
Gross Domestic Product(GDP)(per capita at current prices)(US$)(2000)[2]	2,711
GDP per capita (Purchasing Power Standards* in euros)(as of end 1999)[1]	5,786
GDP per capita (Purchasing Power Standards)(per cent of EU average)(1999)[1]	27
GDP at current prices (billion euros)(1999)[1]	5.7
Inflation rate, annual average (June 2000**)[1]	2.7
Appreciation/depreciation of national currency against the euro/Ecu (2001) (1997=100)[3]	118.87

Sources: [1] Eurostat (2000); [2] IMF (2000) *World Economic Outlook Database*, September; [3] Datastream.

Notes: * Eurostat defines Purchasing Power Standards as an artificial currency to enable correct comparison of volume of goods and services produced by different countries. Figures have been calculated using the population figures from National Accounts, which may differ from those used in demographic statistics.
** Moving 12-month average rate of change.

When Latvia restored its independence from the Soviet Union in August 1991, the country still possessed the remnant institutions and practices of central planning, a disintegrating economic infrastructure and many large and unprofitable state-run industries that were narrowly adapted to service the Soviet command economy. Similar to some of its Central and Eastern European counterparts, Latvia realized that dramatic restructuring of its economy and reorientation away from the ailing Soviet state was necessary to ensure its political autonomy and achieve economic prosperity.

Latvia began to restructure its economy by

- adopting its own currency, the lat, and by
- instituting macroeconomic stabilization by implementing tight monetary and fiscal policies. Additionally, Latvia instituted a price liberalization programme in connection with its stabilization programme from July 1992 to July 1993. However, Latvia had a delayed privatization process because of the slow development of the necessary institutions and legal framework, late parliamentary elections and the adoption of citizenship laws.

Latvia does not see itself merely as a beneficiary of EU funds, but recognizes the expectations of being able to contribute both concepts and plans that will benefit both Latvia and the EU at large. Latvia does not consider its small size to be an obstacle in forwarding and taking strategic decisions and points to existing EU member countries, such as Belgium and Luxembourg, as examples of the ability to contribute despite size.

PROCESS OF EU ACCESSION

Accession talks reflect the progress of Latvia's ability to meet the EU entry requirements. Membership of the EU has its drawbacks, even though it will open a much larger market for Latvia. The economic progress, which has been taking place in the late 1990s and during the year 2000, may not be adequate to survive the intense intra-EU longer-run competition. This is because Latvia's economic expansion has been mainly in the following areas:

■ non-tradable services;

■ foreign direct investment in mainly low-technology industries;

■ monopoly in transit trade.

Moreover, the monopoly in transit trade is itself constrained and threatened by geographical limitations and a growing over-capacity. Costs may be incurred because present EU members are calling for accession countries to bear a greater burden (or receive less transfers) towards the expense of enlargement.

In October 1998 the European Commission published a first set of regular reports on the applicant countries, which was submitted to the Vienna European Council. In October 1999 a second set of progress reports was made, which was submitted to the Helsinki European Committee. Subsequently, the Helsinki European Council recommended that accession negotiations with Latvia were to commence in the year 2000 (*see* Table 11.2).

Table 11.2 Evolution of the relationship between Latvia and the EU

Date	Stage of application	Additional comments
June 1995	Europe Agreement signed[1]	The legal basis for the relations with the EU
October 1995	Official application for EU membership submitted	
July 1997	European Commission Opinion received (just before Luxembourg presidency) for all the applicant countries	

Date	Stage of application	Additional comments
December 1997	The European Council decided to open negotiations (accession negotiations were recommended with six other applicant countries but Latvia was excluded)[2]	To be distinguished from accession negotiations that were recommended to be opened in December 1999
December 1997	European Council decided to initiate an accession process on March 1998[1]	
October 1998	The Commission issued its first Regular Report on Latvia[3]	Aimed at Vienna European Council
June 1999	Latvia presented an amended National Programme for the Adoption of the *Acquis* (NPAA)[4]	Established a schedule for meeting the goals set out in the Accession Partnerships
October 1999	The Commission issued its second Regular Report on Latvia[3]	Aimed at Helsinki European Council
October 1999	European Commission recommended member states to open accession negotiations with Latvia[1]	
December 1999	EU member states endorsed accession negotiations with Latvia at Helsinki Summit[1]	
November 2000	The Commission issued its third Regular Report on Latvia[3]	

Sources: [1] European Commission (1999) Directorate-General Enlargement; [2] Luxembourg European Council (1997) *Presidency Conclusions*, December; [3] European Commission (2000), *Regular Report on Latvia's Progress Towards Accession*, November; [4] European Commission (1999) *Accession Partnership for Latvia*, Directorate-General Enlargement, December.

MEETING EU REQUIREMENTS FOR ENTRY

Meeting political criteria

Latvia 'continues to'[1] fulfil the political criteria laid down by the Copenhagen European Council in June 1993. A number of shortcomings are observed, however, which can be summarized as follows:

- The strong delay and the lack of political consensus in implementing the reform of the public administration constitute a big obstacle to the efficient functioning of the Parliament and of the civil service.

- The absence of a unified public service results in a lack of well-qualified and experienced personnel.

- The legal system is still not up to the required standard and has to be improved. Moreover, the process of implementing the judicial system is still slow.

- Important laws such as Law on State Agencies and Law on Institutional Structure of the Public Administration are still awaiting approval by the Parliament.

- There is no co-ordination between court bailiffs and the court system. Judges are not well qualified and there are long delays in court proceedings.

- Corruption remains a serious matter. Sufficient reform of the legal framework is still not in place and anti-corruption measures are rather general and lack organization.

- In terms of civil and political rights, Latvia made important improvements, though the trafficking of women and children for prostitution abroad is increasing. Women often face discrimination in the workplace in terms of hiring and pay.

- The alignment of refugee and asylum legislation along international standards needs to be addressed. The health and sanitary conditions of some prisons and centres for illegal immigrants are still not up to the EU standard.

- Finally, little progress has been made in the implementation of laws in support of minority rights and their protection. The process of integration of non-citizens faces obstacles in terms of language and profession. The naturalization process and the Latvia language scheme have to be improved. There is no legislation for the protection of the rights of the mentally ill.

Meeting economic criteria

Latvia has the hallmarks of a 'market economy', which is a requirement stipulated in the European Council in Copenhagen in June 1993.[2] Macroeconomic stability has been reached purely as a result of a strengthening banking sector. However, some improvements and further progress are required in the following areas:

- The process of elimination of barriers to market entry and exit is in need of further action. In particular, the legislation on competition policy has to be put in place and bankruptcy rules have to be strengthened. Domestically owned enterprises are performing well, but they need a better restructuring in terms of ownership entitlements and rights regarding transferability of assets.

- The fiscal consolidation is proceeding slowly. Macroeconomic stability in terms of public and external finances has to be more solidly ensured. The country's programme of privatization was slowed down during the years 1998–2000 and some of the most valuable assets are still in the hands of the state.

- The problem of the external account has to be seriously addressed. The current account deficit stood at around 10 per cent of the GDP in 1999. Small and medium-sized firms experience difficulties in raising finance. Lending institutions, such as banks, demand hefty collateral, especially from those setting up new businesses. The role of financial intermediaries has to be substantially improved.

In line with the Copenhagen Criteria, Latvia can count on a broad consensus on economic policy. The new coalition government is maintaining the economic strategies previously adopted.

Meeting obligations of membership

Latvia has opened 16 chapters of the *acquis* for negotiations, of which nine have been provisionally closed (*see* Table 11.3).

Table 11.3 Latvia: state of negotiations on chapters of the *acquis communautaire* (at start of 2001)

Chapter	Title	State of play	Date
1	Free movement of goods	~	
2	Freedom of movement for persons	~	
3	Freedom to provide services	O	
4	Free movement of capital	O	
5	Company law	O	
6	Competition policy	O	
7	Agriculture	~	
8	Fisheries	O	
9	Transport policy	O	
10	Taxation	~	
11	Economic and monetary union	✓	Nov. 2000
12	Statistics	✓	May 2000
13	Social policy and employment	~	
14	Energy	~	
15	Industrial policy	✓	Nov. 2000
16	Small and medium-sized undertakings	✓	May 2000
17	Science and research	✓	May 2000
18	Education and training	✓	May 2000
19	Telecommunications and information technologies	~	
20	Culture and audio-visual policy	O	
21	Regional policy and co-ordination of structural instruments	~	
22	Environment	~	
23	Consumers and health protection	✓	Nov. 2000
24	Co-operation in the fields of justice and home affairs	~	

Chapters	Title	State of play	Date
25	Customs union	~	
26	External relations	✓	Nov. 2000
27	Common foreign and security policy	✓	May 2000
28	Financial control	~	
29	Financial and budgetary provisions	~	
30	Institutions		
31	Other		
Total chapters opened		16	(Start of 2001)
Total chapters provisionally closed		9	(Start of 2001)

O = chapter opened, under negotiation; ✓ = chapter provisionally closed; ~ = chapter not yet opened to negotiation.

Source: European Commission (2000) Directorate-General Enlargement.

TIMING OF ACCESSION

Latvia might be among the first round of the applicant countries to join the EU despite the fact that:

- its accession negotiations only started in 2000, whereas six applicant countries commenced their accession negotiations in 1998;

- it had satisfied only nine chapters of the *acquis* by the beginning of 2001.

Suffice it to say that the argument of the 'first entry wave' rests upon the assumption that a first wave of countries could and possibly would be allowed to join the EU around 2004/2005[3] or close to that date.

Nevertheless, the rationale behind the timing of 2004/2005 rests only on a statement of the President of the EU in November 2000 made at a press conference. This statement was made at the time of the publication of the 2000 series of the Commission Regular Reports. Mr. Prodi was quoted as saying that they 'would do their best' to enable candidates to join the EU after the start of 2004 before the next European Parliament elections (in June 2004).[4]

Notes

1 European Commission (2000) *Regular Report on Latvia's Progress Towards Accession*, November. See the discussion in Chapter 2.

2 Ibid., p. 24. See also Chapter 2.

3 See Chapter 2, Patterns of important EU decisions, page 30.

4 Ibid.

Lithuania

OVERVIEW

Lithuania is a little behind some of its fellow applicant countries in its preparation for joining the EU. The country has satisfied only seven out of its 16 open chapters of the *acquis communautaire* which is part of the requirement for entry into the EU.

The European Commission's directorate-general responsible for EU enlargement has identified certain shortcomings in Lithuania's accession. These were highlighted in the Commission's 1999 short and medium-term strategy paper on Lithuania, which assesses Lithuania's readiness for accession.[1]

Lithuania's agricultural sector is still in need of restructuring and is still being subsidized by state aid, even where businesses are failing. The country's food-processing industry requires reform, liberalization of the market and discouragement of subsidies, in order for it to follow market powers. Equally in need of attention is Lithuania's energy sector and matters related to the environment (more details are given below).

Table 12.1 Overview of the Lithuanian economy

Population average (millions)(1999)[1]	3.700
Gross Domestic Product(GDP)(per capita at current prices)(US$)(2000)[2]	3,007
GDP per capita (Purchasing Power Standards* in euros)(as of end 1999)[1]	6,169
GDP per capita (Purchasing Power Standards)(per cent of EU average)(1999)[1]	29
GDP at current prices (billion euros)(1999)[1]	10
Inflation rate, annual average (January–June 2000**)[1]	0.8
Appreciation/depreciation of national currency against the euro/Ecu (2001) (1997=100)[3]	133.13

Sources: [1] Eurostat (2000); [2] IMF (2000) *World Economic Outlook Database*, September; [3] Datastream.

Notes: * Eurostat defines Purchasing Power Standards as an artificial currency to enable correct comparison of volume of goods and services produced by different countries. Figures have been calculated using the population figures from National Accounts, which may differ from those used in demographic statistics.
** Moving 12-month average rate of change.

By and large in both quality and quantity Lithuania still needs to improve its legislative institutions and personnel used in the fighting of crime, particularly in corruption, money laundering, trafficking of narcotics, and counterfeiting. Another area of concern is the control of national borders – controlling immigration to inhibit illegal entrance is vital. Legislation to improve the legal pace of asylum seekers and legal help for refugees must also be offered.

In addition Lithuania needs to address the problem of administration and policing of corruption, particularly in the fields of customs, intellectual property rights and data protection. It needs to repeal its restrictions on the investment and operation of pension and insurance companies, especially those that are foreign owned, and its VAT structure still needs to be implemented.

PROCESS OF EU ACCESSION

Lithuania sees its application for EU membership as a means of strengthening its security, as well as enjoying the enhanced economic benefits from free trade with the EU, and also benefiting from any transfers it may receive.

The Government that came into power in May 1999 left office shortly thereafter (in late October 1999). A different Government came to power in November 1999, which had the backing of the Lithuanian Parliament (the *Seimas*) and reiterated the intention to take the country into the EU.

Table 12.2 Evolution of the relationship between Lithuania and the EU

Date	Stage of application	Additional comments
June 1995	Europe Agreement signed	The legal basis for the relations with the EU
December 1995	Official application for EU membership submitted	
July 1997	European Commission Opinion received (just before the start of Luxembourg presidency) for all the applicant countries	It was negative for Lithuania (six countries received a 'yes' five countries received a 'no'), saying Lithuania needed more time
December 1997	The European Council decided to open negotiations (accession negotiations were recommended with six other applicant countries but Lithuania was excluded)[1]	To be distinguished from accession negotiations that were recommended to be opened in December 1999
March 1998	First Accession Partnerships were decided between the European Commission and Lithuania	Set out short and medium-term strategies and priorities as they pertain to the *acquis*
October 1998	The Commission issued its first Regular Report on Lithuania	Aimed at Vienna European Council. The regular reports give an overview of developments in the applicant country
May 1999	Lithuania presented an amended National Programme for the Adoption of the *Acquis* (NPAA)	Established a schedule for meeting the goals set out in the Accession Partnerships

Date	Stage of application	Additional comments
October 1999	European Commission recommended member states to open accession negotiations with Lithuania	
October 1999	The Commission issued its second Regular Report on Lithuania	Aimed at Helsinki European Council
December 1999	EU member states endorsed accession negotiations with Lithuania at Helsinki Summit	
December 1999	An amended Accession Partnership adopted	
May 2000	Lithuania presented an amended National Programme for the Adoption of the *Acquis* (NPAA)[2]	
November 2000	The Commission issued its third Regular Report on Lithuania	

Sources: [1] Luxembourg European Council (1997) *Presidency Conclusions*, December; [2] European Commission (1999) *Accession Partnership for Lithuania*, Directorate-General Enlargement, December.

Notes: (1) European Commission (1999) Directorate-General Enlargement.
(2) European Commission (2000) *Regular Report on Lithuania's Progress Towards Accession*, November.

To meet EU Directives, Lithuania requires a rearrangement of its environmental legislature. In addition, it must develop its financing and enforce legislation in all realms of environmental protection, particularly for radioactive products and by-products. This enforcement of the law must be imposed by local and central government.

MEETING EU REQUIREMENTS FOR ENTRY

The conditions to be fulfilled for admittance into the EU as stated in the Copenhagen European Council in June 1993 are analysed below.

Meeting political criteria

Lithuania 'continues to fulfil' the political requirements demanded by the Copenhagen Council. Lithuania now has a reliable structure, which means that the country can ensure democracy and the rule of law. There are, nevertheless, several areas that still require addressing. These are the need to decrease corruption and to restructure the legal institutions.[2]

Public administration and civil service laws are in the process of being passed. The necessary laws have been put in place regarding the register and status of civil servants, i.e. how freely they can move between departments and what jobs can be taken by people appointed by the government rather than by those who have worked their way up. This is only a start. The process is unlikely to be fully completed for a further four years (to 2004). More efforts are needed in this area.

The state is trying to simplify its internal structure and workings, with the aim of preventing different ministries performing similar tasks. For example, in October 2000 it was decided by the Parliament to combine the Ministry of Public Administration Reforms and Local Administration Reforms into the Ministry of Interior. To improve the working of the Government, this policy needs to be expanded.

For civil servants the Government has initiated a training programme, the National Strategy of Training of Civil Servants in Preparation for EU Membership, which is run by the Lithuanian Institute of Public Administration (LIPA). This is a short-run programme that has been put in place in response to the 1999 demands of the European Commission, set in the strategy paper entitled *Accession Partnership for Lithuania*.[3]

The Lithuanian Government is improving the organizational ability of its European Committee, which deals with issues concerning the potential accession to the EU. In May 2000 the Government established some 17 Law Harmonization Commissions to bring its laws further into line with those of the rest of the EU.

All these measures – especially the progress being made with the law on public administration and the law on the civil service (with increased importance placed on how officials are appointed) – mean that the civil service is mostly free from government influences. Nevertheless, there are still changes to be made to improve the civil service, including in pay, training, and the possibility of greater co-operation between departments.

There are also constant changes in the justice system with problems that need to be solved. Each case is taking too long and there are too many cases in the queue, with very few qualified judges. In some cases the court rulings and decisions are not obeyed. However, lack of funds means there have been few positive developments.

In December 1999 the Constitutional Court decided that the judges working at the Ministry of Justice were not independent in contradiction to the constitution – and that the law should be modified to correct this.

Meeting economic criteria

Lithuania has made great efforts to transform its former centrally planned economy into one based on free market principles. Housing, land and small-to-medium-sized enterprises were quickly privatized. The latter, alongside with favourable trade conditions, have stimulated investment. Since 1995 Lithuania's macroeconomic position has been positive, with lower inflation and a reduction of national debt. These were in turn facilitated by political stability. By 1993 the prices on most goods had been liberalized, with certain government restrictions remaining – but being gradually phased out – on rents, utilities and transport.

Lithuania still needs to make progress in the following areas:

- stabilizing its fiscal deficit;
- finalizing its planned privatization and bank restructuring programmes;
- stimulating competitive markets through small businesses;
- maintaining land cataloguing to meet the target of completion by December 2000, while backing land market improvements;
- modernizing the banking system.

Although Lithuania's legal system is quite independent it suffers from a lack of fully qualified professionals. In turn this adversely affects the overall efficiency of the legal process especially in relatively new areas such as commercial law.

Prices in Lithuania have remained stable due to both administrative controls on certain items (for example, rents and electricity) and the existence of a currency board that restricts the printing on money to control the budget. However, this tight fiscal stance has meant a contraction in credit that has been passed on to businesses. Lithuania's national currency – the *litas* – has appreciated relative to Lithuania's neighbouring countries' currencies, with the result that exporters' products are becoming less competitive.

Lithuania is making progress in meeting the economic requirements stipulated by the European Council in Copenhagen.[4] The economy has been recovering, partly because of an improved external demand. However, there are some areas that have to be improved:

- Market entry and exit remain an ordeal. The Russian crisis has increased the number of bankruptcies, so creating a backlog. The legislation has to be strengthened and the procedures need to be speeded up.

- Macroeconomic instability – in terms of public and external finances – still exists, particularly in the medium term. Consumer price inflation is low, but this is because of a weak domestic demand.

- The financial sector is undeveloped. There are still strict prudential rules and financial institutions are unwilling to provide finance to non-government borrowers. The entire sector is in need of restructuring. The interest rate level is quite high due to economic volatility.

The Russian crisis and its impact on the Lithuanian economy, it has also strengthened the general consensus on economic policy.

Meeting obligations of membership

Lithuania still has a history of recurring fiscal deficits, despite its commitment to their elimination. Deficits have been brought on:

- internally: from a complex system of numerous exemptions (especially on goods) and poor revenue collection, because of inefficient and inexperienced administration;
- externally: from its own banking crisis in 1995, which was bailed out with public funds, and from the Russian financial crisis in 1998.

Other subjects that require particular attention in the chapters of the *acquis* are the following:

- Consumer rights – new laws have to be enforced to improve consumer rights, coupled with the introduction of consumer watchdogs.
- Intellectual and industrial property rights – legislature and border controls have to be reinforced to prevent the illegal sale and production of goods and services.
- Free movement of goods – legislation to raise standards of products has to be improved, supported by market inspection.
- Free movement of capital – red tape on inflows and outflows of capital has to be decreased, to increase the efficient flow of inward investment.
- Competition – anti-trust laws have to be enacted and markets have to be monitored through the Competition Council.
- Telecommunications – a self-governing regulatory organization has to be created.
- Taxation – the taxation system has to be standardized.
- Agriculture – regulation of the sector has to be maintained, while focusing on external borders.
- Transport – safety at sea has to be improved.

Finally, Lithuania's energy sector is not fully independent of state ownership and the country is still too reliant on its nuclear industry to supply its electricity needs. The EU has encouraged Lithuania to decommission its Ignalina Unit 1 nuclear plant because of safety concerns. All present and future power plants must be built to avoid damage to the environment, and a programme of radioactive management must be instigated. Additionally, the EU is encouraging Lithuania to seek diversification in energy production by overhauling its conventional power industry. However, Lithuania has limited fossil fuels and hydro-electrical reserves, and is exclusively dependent on Russia for gas supplies.

To date, of 16 open chapters, Lithuania has provisionally closed only seven (*see* Table 12.3).

Table 12.3 Lithuania: state of negotiations on chapters of the *acquis communautaire* (at start of 2001)

Chapter	Title	State of play	Date
1	Free movement of goods	~	
2	Freedom of movement for persons	~	
3	Freedom to provide services	O	
4	Free movement of capital	O	
5	Company law	O	
6	Competition policy	O	
7	Agriculture	~	
8	Fisheries	~	
9	Transport policy	O	
10	Taxation	~	
11	Economic and monetary union	~	
12	Statistics	✓	May 2000
13	Social policy and employment	O	
14	Energy	~	
15	Industrial policy	✓	
16	Small and medium-sized undertakings	✓	May 2000
17	Science and research	✓	May 2000
18	Education and training	✓	May 2000
19	Telecommunications and information technologies	O	
20	Culture and audio-visual policy	[✓]	
21	Regional policy and co-ordination of structural instruments	~	
22	Environment	O	
23	Consumers and health protection	~	
24	Co-operation in the fields of justice and home affairs	~	
25	Customs union	~	
26	External relations	✓	May 2000
27	Common foreign and security policy	✓	Nov. 2000
28	Financial control	~	
29	Financial and budgetary provisions	~	
30	Institutions		
31	Other		
Total chapters opened		16	(Start of 2001)
Total chapters provisionally closed		7	(Start of 2001)

O = chapter opened, under negotiation; ✓ = chapter provisionally closed; [✓] = chapter for which the Commission has proposed provisional closure; ~ = chapter not yet opened to negotiation.

Source: European Commission (2000) Directorate-General Enlargement.

TIMING OF ACCESSION

Lithuania has a much smaller ethnic Russian minority than its Estonian and Latvian counterparts, because it was less industrialized and militarized during Soviet times. Because of this Lithuania has not had the same tensions that Estonia and Latvia have had with their own Russian minorities. As a result, Lithuania has had better relations with Russia than the other Baltic States.

There are, however, sensitivities present in Russo-Lithuanian affairs that can affect and be affected by Lithuania's EU accession. The EU has called on Lithuania to begin demarcation proceedings with Kaliningrad – a highly militarized Russian province. Kaliningrad is not contiguous with Russia itself, and at present Lithuania allows Russia passage through Lithuanian territory to maintain links with Kaliningrad.

Another major obstacle to Lithuania's EU membership is its Ignalina nuclear plant. The EU has identified its desire for the plant to be decommissioned because of environmental and safety concerns, since it has a similar design to the Chernobyl nuclear plant. The European Bank for Reconstruction and Development (EBRD) is the financial co-ordinator for Ignalina's decommissioning. The Lithuanian government has indicated to the EU that the cost of closure could reach $4 billion. The decommissioning of Ignalina is not unique among the accession countries. Nuclear plants at Bohunice in Slovakia and Kozlodui in Bulgaria have also been identified by the EU for closure with EBRD funding. Ignalina's future will affect not only Lithuania but also its neighbours, such as Estonia and Belarus, to whom the plant provides exports of electricity.

Given all the preparation required, the estimated time for Lithuania's accession time could be approximately 2004 entry, or possibly 2005–6.

Notes

1   European Commission (1999) *Accession Partnership for Lithuania*, Directorate-General Enlargement, December.

2   European Commission (2000) *Regular Report on Lithuania's Progress Towards Accession*, November.

3   European Commission (1999) *Accession Partnership for Lithuania*, Directorate-General Enlargement, December.

4   European Commission (2000) *Regular Report on Lithuania's Progress Towards Accession*, November, pp. 22–31.

13

Bulgaria

OVERVIEW

Bulgaria received formal approval by the European Council in December 1999 at the Helsinki Council to open accession negotiations. The country had, however, submitted its application for EU membership in December 1995. In February 2000, during the bilateral intergovernmental conference between Bulgaria and the EU, formal negotiations began for Bulgaria's accession.[1]

Bulgaria has been adhering to a currency board and as a result it has been able to reduce its price inflation significantly. Average inflation over 1999 was 2.6 per cent. However, the increased oil prices and the rise in administered prices pushed inflation to 7.6 per cent by June 2000. Table 13.1 provides some insights into the Bulgarian economy.

Table 13.1 Overview of the Bulgarian economy

Population average (millions)(1999)[1]	8.211
Gross Domestic Product(GDP)(per capita at current prices)(US$)(2000)[2]	1,619
GDP per capita (Purchasing Power Standards* in euros)(1999)[1]	4,749
GDP per capita (Purchasing Power Standards)(per cent of EU average)(1999)[1]	22
GDP at current prices (billion euros)(1999)[1]	11.6
Inflation rate, annual average (as of June 2000**)[1]	7.6
Appreciation/depreciation of national currency against the euro/Ecu (2001) (1997=100)[3]	31687.34

Sources: [1] Eurostat (2000); [2] IMF (2000) *World Economic Outlook Database*, September; [3] Datastream.

Notes: * Eurostat defines Purchasing Power Standards as an artificial currency to enable correct comparison of volume of goods and services produced by different countries. Figures have been calculated using the population figures from National Accounts, which may differ from those used in demographic statistics.
** Moving 12-month average rate of change.

PROCESS OF EU ACCESSION

The stages of Bulgaria's application for EU entry are summarized in Table 13.2. In the light of persistent problems, Bulgaria's hope of an early EU integration is likely to be dashed. It is clear that the pace of reform does not match the EU entry requirements.

The Commission still identifies 'market entry and exit' as a point of concern, casting doubt over the Government's ability to address effectively the problem in the short and medium term. On the other hand, the Bulgarian Government has claimed significant advances through improved insolvency procedures and simplification of the regulatory climate.[2]

Table 13.2 Evolution of the relationship between Bulgaria and the EU

Date	Stages of application	Additional comments
May 1990	Trade and Co-operation agreement signed[1]	
March 1993	Europe Agreement signed[1]	
February 1995	Europe Agreement came into effect[1]	
December 1995	Bulgaria presented its application for membership of the EU[1]	
December 1997	The European Council decided to open negotiations (accession negotiations were recommended with six other applicant countries but Bulgaria was excluded)[2]	To be distinguished from accession negotiations that were recommended to be opened in December 1999
March 1998	First Accession Partnerships decided between the Commission and Bulgaria[2]	Accession Partnership sets out short and medium-term strategies and priorities as they pertain to the *Acquis*
October 1998	The Commission issued its first Regular Report on Bulgaria[3]	Aimed at Vienna European Council
October 1999	The Commission issued its second Regular Report on Bulgaria[3]	Aimed at Helsinki European Council
16 November 1999	Association Council meeting held[3]	
December 1999	EU member states endorsed accession negotiations with Bulgaria at Helsinki Summit	Following a recommendation by the Commission on 13 October 1999
December 1999	An amended Accession Partnership adopted[3]	
15 February 2000	Negotiations officially opened at the bilateral intergovernmental conference[3]	
November 2000	The Commission issued its third Regular Report on Bulgaria[3]	

Sources: [1] European Commission (1997) *Opinion on Bulgaria's Application for Membership of the European Union*, July; [2] European Commission (1999) *Accession Partnership for Bulgaria*, Directorate-General Enlargement, December; [3] European Commission (2000) *Regular Report on Bulgaria's Progress Towards Accession*, November.

A similar reaction on the part of the European Commission can be observed in the financial sector. The Bulgarian Government responded to the Commission's 1999 call for reform with a restructuring of the legal framework to allow banks more flexibility. The government reports that banks are now venturing into higher profit investment. Furthermore the Law on Public Offerings of Securities (31 January 2000) is aimed at the development of the capital markets.[3] Again, the Commission has not been satisfied.

The functioning of the judiciary is certainly below standard. Attempts to address the Commission's concerns include enhanced communications between the Ministry of Justice and the Magistrate Training Centre in order to improve training standards for judges. On the administrative side, technology is to be upgraded, statistical information is to be used to monitor the performance of the judiciary, and higher academic standards are to be applied to the qualifications of the staff.

In reality the judiciary is still in a poor state and previous examples highlight that concrete improvements are expected to occur only in the distant future. For example, the Commission claims that the calls for reform in the 1999 report had not been acted upon in 2000. Furthermore, funding is inadequate to perform the necessary changes.[4] The lack of progress points towards a prolonged accession process.

The *acquis* chapters relating to the internal market cannot be closed without the necessary reforms to the judiciary. Moreover, transition periods are unlikely to be granted for these chapters.

MEETING EU REQUIREMENTS FOR ENTRY

Among the three principle criteria, Bulgaria has only managed to meet the political criteria. The establishment of the currency board has contributed to lowering the level of inflation, but a substantial number of the conditions still remain unfulfilled.

Meeting political criteria

Bulgaria 'continues to meet' the Copenhagen political criteria.[5] However, a concerted attempt is needed if Bulgaria is to satisfy requirements such as the rule of law and involvement in the internal market.

There is insufficient funding for the judiciary and the system itself is poorly managed and outdated. Judges are incompetent in relation to EU standards: while they have a heightened social status, they benefit from corrupt and unacceptable procedures. Significant reforms and modernization are required.

Political problems are also unlikely to be resolved in the near future. New laws have been passed to combat corruption, for example the Council of Europe Civil Law Convention on Corruption. Other priority areas for the Government in customs, taxation authorities, municipalities, the judiciary and the police (addressed in the Civil Service Law, 21 July 1999).[6] Efforts by the Government have not as yet convinced the European Commission, which still identifies the police and the judiciary as the main offenders.[7] Corruption also exists within the university system.

Despite government attempts to address the protection of minorities, especially the position of the Roma, there is little evidence of any form of concrete action. The Roma still live in dilapidated housing, and suffer chronic unemployment and ill health. The minority is excluded from the social benefits system and cannot acquire the necessary healthcare.

Meeting economic criteria

Bulgaria has not fulfilled the requirements of the Copenhagen economic criteria. The country is not yet able to face competitive pressure and market forces that exist in the EU in the medium term. Areas of concern are:

- The insolvency procedure is sluggish and poorly implemented. New companies are prevented from entering, as a result of complex rules and regulations. Also foreign companies are discouraged by the frequency of tax inspections. In addition, many badly performing companies are not closed down – hindering the more competent ventures as well as obstructing the functioning of a competitive market.

- Clearer property rights are required.

- Problems persist in directing savings towards investment. The achievements here have been less than impressive. In 1999 13.5 per cent of GDP was directed towards investment – not a high amount given that in 1995 the figure was 12.7 per cent. The financial market is still in an elementary stage – there is little trading activity due to the high costs of the brokers and illiquid conditions. The magnitude of the spread between the borrowing rate of interest and the rate earned on deposit accounts is around 9 per cent.

The external debt is particularly large, exposing the country to shocks from abroad. At the close of 1999 the level of external debt reached 79.8 per cent of GDP. While a decrease in debt would lessen the chances of fiscal crisis, Bulgaria needs to take due care in its strategy.

The problem of foreign debt, nevertheless, should not detract funding from infrastructure development, for this would have a negative impact upon economic growth. The debt should be serviced primarily with privatization revenues. It should be noted that it is not necessary to decrease the public debt prior to accession, hence Bulgaria should be careful not to neglect other issues.

Meeting obligations of membership

During the Portuguese presidency (January–June 2000) Bulgaria opened six chapters of the *acquis* for negotiations. These were:

- science and research
- education and training
- small and medium-sized enterprises
- common foreign and security policy
- culture and audio-visual policy
- external relations.

The first four of the above listed chapters were provisionally closed by June 2000 (*see* Table 13.3). Subsequently, negotiations on a further five chapters commenced during the French presidency (July–December 2000). These were:

- free movement of capital
- company law
- statistics
- telecoms
- consumers and health protection.

Table 13.3 Bulgaria: state of negotiations on chapters of the *acquis communautaire* (at start of 2001)

Chapter	Title	State of play	Date
1	Free movement of goods	~	
2	Freedom of movement for persons	~	
3	Freedom to provide services	~	
4	Free movement of capital	O	
5	Company law	O	
6	Competition policy	~	
7	Agriculture	~	
8	Fisheries	~	
9	Transport policy	~	
10	Taxation	~	
11	Economic and monetary union	~	
12	Statistics	✓	Nov. 2000
13	Social policy and employment	~	
14	Energy	~	
15	Industrial policy	~	
16	Small and medium-sized undertakings	✓	May 2000

Chapter	Title	State of play	Date
17	Science and research	✓	May 2000
18	Education and training	✓	May 2000
19	Telecommunications and information technologies	O	
20	Culture and audio-visual policy	✓	Nov. 2000
21	Regional policy and co-ordination of structural instruments	~	
22	Environment	~	
23	Consumers and health protection	✓	Nov. 2000
24	Co-operation in the fields of justice and home affairs	~	
25	Customs union	~	
26	External relations	✓	Nov. 2000
27	Common foreign and security policy	✓	Nov. 2000
28	Financial control	~	
29	Financial and budgetary provisions	~	
30	Institutions		
31	Other		
Total chapters opened		11	(Start of 2001)
Total chapters provisionally closed		8	(Start of 2001)

O = chapter opened, under negotiation; ✓ = chapter provisionally closed; ~ = chapter not yet opened to negotiation.

Source: European Commission (2000) Directorate-General Enlargement.

TIMING OF ACCESSION

The persistent lack of progress described above suggests that preparations for accession will take longer than the Bulgarian Government envisages. Bulgaria is unlikely to enter the EU until 2007/2008 at the earliest.

Notes

1   European Commission (2000) *Regular Report on Bulgaria's Progress Towards Accession*, November, p.12.

2   Bulgarian Ministry of Foreign Affairs (2000) *Progress Report on the Political Criteria*, October.

3   Bulgarian Ministry of Foreign Affairs (2000) *Progress Report on the Economic Criteria*, October.

4   European Commission (2000) *Regular Report on Bulgaria's Progress Towards Accession*, November.

5   Ibid.

6   Bulgarian Ministry of Foreign Affairs (2000) *Progress Report on the Political Criteria*, October.

7   European Commission (2000) *Regular Report on Bulgaria's Progress Towards Accession*, November.

Romania

OVERVIEW

Following its application to join the EU, Romania has attempted to demonstrate its commitment to EU accession. The country has taken some steps and has introduced reforms in a few areas, for example:

■ respecting the right to strike;

■ respecting the right to demonstrate;

■ protecting the rights of the Hungarian minority;

■ improving the position of the orphans in care.

However, while the country is edging closer to its goal of EU membership, it has to make a compelling case for entry by adopting an accelerating schedule of reform.

Table 14.1 provides some insights into the Romanian economy. The development of human capital in Romania is endangered by a low participation rate of young people in higher education, increased poverty, growing income inequality and the deterioration in the quality of social services and infrastructures. The country is in desperate need of foreign capital in all sectors of its economy.

Table 14.1 Overview of the Romanian economy

Population average (millions)(1999)[1]	22.458
Gross Domestic Product(GDP)(per capita at current prices)(US$)(2000)[2]	1,601
GDP per capita (Purchasing Power Standards* in euros)(as of end 1999)[1]	5,682
GDP per capita (Purchasing Power Standards)(per cent of EU average)(1999)[1]	27
GDP at current prices (billion euros)(1999)[1]	31.9
Inflation rate, annual average (June 2000**)[1]	50.0
Appreciation/depreciation of national currency against the euro/Ecu (2001) (1997=100)[3]	21.22

Sources: [1] Eurostat (2000); [2] IMF (2000) *World Economic Outlook Database*, September; [3] Datastream.

Notes: * Eurostat defines Purchasing Power Standards as an artificial currency to enable correct comparison of volume of goods and services produced by different countries. Figures have been calculated using the population figures from National Accounts, which may differ from those used in demographic statistics.
** Moving 12-month average rate of change.

Since 1998 the European Commission has concluded that Romania 'continues to fulfil' the political criteria as part of the accession requirement.

Alas, after a decade of painful but largely unfruitful reforms, the country has not staged a sweeping recovery from the economic stagnation of the socialist era and does not portray an image of a market economy on a par with its neighbours Hungary and Slovakia.

PROCESS OF EU ACCESSION

Part of the reason for the slow progress Romania has made towards conforming with the EU requirements (*see* Table 14.2) has been the inability of its Government to undertake the necessary reforms. This in turn was partly due to the constraints of the ruling coalition government, which had been in power until November 2000. For example, the Romanian parliamentary session was quite inactive during 1999 – having passed a mere one-ninth of the required total (only 59 of 453 laws and ordinances) that was scheduled for the year 1999. This state of affairs has persisted through 2000 until the November 2000 parliamentary elections took place.

Due to the unstable nature of its coalition, the Romanian Government has been attempting to force legislation through by issuing ordinances under emergency criteria that take immediate effect and, therefore, escape proper preliminary debate. This is a source of legislative instability that is not in compliance with EU standards.

Nevertheless, despite the use of such emergency ordinances, the implementation of the reform is still being delayed. Lack of an effective coalition is not the only reason for this problem. Deficient databases and unqualified administrative personnel are further hampering the progress.

Table 14.2 Evolution of the relationship between Romania and the EU

Date	Stage of application	Additional comments
February 1993	Europe Agreement signed	The legal basis for the relations with the EU (known also as Association Agreement)
February 1995	Europe Agreement came into force	
June 1995	Official application for EU membership submitted	
December 1997	The European Council decided to open negotiations (Accession negotiations were recommended with six other applicant countries but Romania was excluded)[1]	To be distinguished from accession negotiations that were recommended to be opened in December 1999
March 1998	First Accession Partnerships decided between the European Commission and Romania	Set out short and medium-term strategies and priorities as they pertain to the *acquis*
October 1998	The Commission issued its first Regular Report on Romania	Aimed at Vienna European Council
October 1999	The Commission issued its second Regular Report on Romania	Aimed at Helsinki European Council

Date	Stage of application	Additional comments
October 1999	The Commission recommended member states to open negotiations with Romania	
December 1999	An amended Accession Partnership adopted	
December 1999	Member states endorsed the European Commission recommendation to formally open accession negotiations with Romania	Agreed at the Helsinki Summit
May 2000	Romania presented an amended National Programme for the Adoption of the Acquis (NPAA)	
November 2000	The Commission issued its third Regular Report on Romania	

Sources: European Commission (2000) *Regular Report on Romania's Progress Towards Accession*, November; [1] Luxembourg European Council (1997) *Presidency Conclusions*, December; European Commission (1999) *Accession Partnership for Romania*, Directorate-General Enlargement, December.

MEETING EU REQUIREMENTS FOR ENTRY

While Romania has had every intention of introducing reforms and meeting the EU entry requirement, this has proved challenging in practice.

Meeting political criteria

The European Commission accepts that Romania has a functioning and responsible democracy and that there is the prevalence of law and order in the country. The local election held in June 2000 and the parliamentary and presidential election held in November 2000 proved the existence of democracy in Romania. Nevertheless, there are still areas of concern:

- the continued corruption;
- the problems of gypsies and a corresponding lack of funding to alleviate the situation;
- the efficient functioning of an independent judiciary system.

The situation *via-à-vis* childcare in Romania still remains of particular concern to the European Union.

Meeting economic criteria

Romania has certainly been a laggard in the creation of a market economy and does not have the hallmarks of one.[1] This is largely due to persistent macroeconomic instability and slow progress with structural reforms. There is also a lack of responsible institutions and the relevant legislature to enforce the necessary measures.

At the macroeconomic level, Romania recorded a number of improvements over the period 1999–2000. The current account deficit was substantially reduced and fell close to zero. Accordingly, external obligations were met in full and in good time. Official reserves were also rebuilt. Despite these positive developments, the overall macroeconomic position deteriorated.[2]

The level of GDP growth continued its former negative trend of the 1990s pattern in 1999. Only in the first half of 2000 was this trend reversed, and then unemployment rose.

Despite a tight monetary policy pursued in 1999 and 2000, price inflation in 2000 again rose to the same level as the previous year – at around 50 per cent. While failing to achieve its objective, the Government's monetary policy proved rather costly for the country. The inter-bank rate in September 2000 rose above the 50 per cent mark (even though it was falling throughout the year).

The medium-term sustainability of fiscal policy in Romania thus remains in doubt. Priorities for the country are:

- to enhance financial discipline within state-owned enterprises;
- to restructure and modernize the system of management of public finances;
- to overhaul the social security, pension and health care systems;
- to establish a tax structure that would encourage compliance and boost business creation.

Market entry in Romania has become more difficult, while market exit does not match a satisfactory standard. In spite of the establishment of a better bankruptcy law, its implementation is poorly managed.

Some 60 per cent of the output comes from the private enterprise sector and around 30–40 per cent is within the black market economy. State ownership of the enterprise sector still remains at a high level. The pace of privatization of large companies has been slow. This would prevent Romania competing effectively in the 'market economy' of the EU.

There is legal uncertainty and unclear property rights with an underdeveloped financial system. Romania suffers from a lack of opportunities for the development of private businesses and foreign capital investments. This in turn inhibits a more rapid economic recovery.

Restructuring of industrial production is another priority for Romania, since modernization of the enterprise sector is a building block for competitiveness for the country's economy.

The agricultural sector is in need of transformation and must carry out such challenging tasks as the replacement of obsolete capital stock, the introduction of solid property rights and the establishment of functioning market institutions.

Some 60 per cent of Romania's external trade flows (both exports and imports) are with the EU. However, the significant income disparity between Romania and the EU orients the pattern of trade towards labour-intensive products. Competitive advantage in Romania lies in subcontracting within industries such as textiles and footwear, which rely on cheap labour for their businesses.

Meeting obligations of membership

Romania still has to make a considerable effort to satisfy all the EU requirements for entry. As Table 14.3 shows, the country has satisfied only six out of the 31 chapters of the *acquis communautaire*. The country has opened a total of nine chapters of the *acquis*, which is below that of its fellow candidates.

Table 14.3 Romania: state of negotiations on chapters of the *acquis communautaire* (at start of 2001)

Chapter	Title	State of play	Date
1	Free movement of goods	~	
2	Freedom of movement for persons	~	
3	Freedom to provide services	~	
4	Free movement of capital	~	
5	Company law	~	
6	Competition policy	O	
7	Agriculture	~	
8	Fisheries	~	
9	Transport policy	~	
10	Taxation	~	
11	Economic and monetary union	~	
12	Statistics	✓	Nov. 2000
13	Social policy and employment	~	
14	Energy	~	
15	Industrial policy	~	
16	Small and medium-sized undertakings	✓	May 2000
17	Science and research	✓	May 2000

Chapter	Title	State of play	Date
18	Education and training	✓	May 2000
19	Telecommunications and information technologies	O	
20	Culture and audio-visual policy	O	
21	Regional policy and co-ordination of structural instruments	~	
22	Environment	~	
23	Consumers and health protection	~	
24	Co-operation in the fields of justice and home affairs	~	
25	Customs union	~	
26	External relations	✓	May 2000
27	Common foreign and security policy	✓	May 2000
28	Financial control	~	
29	Financial and budgetary provisions	~	
30	Institutions		
31	Other		
Total chapters opened		9	(Start of 2001)
Total chapters provisionally closed		6	(Start of 2001)

O = chapter opened, under negotiation; ✓ = chapter provisionally closed; ~ = chapter not yet opened to negotiation.

Source: European Commission (2000) Directorate-General Enlargement.

TIMING OF ACCESSION

Romania may have to remain in the waiting room for a considerable length of time. In terms of preparation, it lags behind some of the other countries whose accession negotiations began in 2000.

The timing of accession for Romania depends on two variables:

■ the timing of the second round;

■ the speed of its own preparations and introduction of the necessary reforms.

As the picture looks at present, and at the pace of its current progression, Romania may even miss the second round.

After a decade of painful but largely unfruitful reforms the country has not staged a sweeping recovery from the economic stagnation of the socialist era and does not portray an image of a healthy and buoyant market economy on a par with its neighbours Hungary and Slovakia. The next ten years should be more productive than the last ten years to ensure Romania's eventual EU entry.

Notes

1   European Commission (2000) *Regular Report on Romania's Progress Towards Accession*, November.

2   In 1999 and the first half of 2000.

15

Turkey

OVERVIEW

Among the 13 applicants reviewed in this book, Turkey was the last country to be declared an official candidate for full membership of the EU. Turkey's future will undoubtedly be radically affected by this development. However, as yet Turkey has not been given the go-ahead to start accession negotiations with the European Commission.

Turkey's quest for EU membership has been long-standing (*see* Table 15.2) – dating back to 1987. Indeed the relationship with the EU began with the signing of the Association Agreement as long ago as 1963. During the 1980s and 1990s Turkey's accession to the EU was continually delayed on the grounds that the country's workings and practices were not found to be compatible with those of the EU. Finally, in 1999 the EU chose to declare Turkey as an official candidate. However, this only enabled the country to commence pre-accession preparatory work. Given the nature of both the political and economic system in Turkey, actual accession may be a long process.

Table 15.1 presents some of the main economic indicators for the country.

Table 15.1 Overview of the Turkish economy

Population average (millions)(1999)[1]	64.330
Gross Domestic Product(GDP)(per capita at current prices)(US$)(2000)[2]	2,943
GDP per capita (Purchasing Power Standards* in euros)(as of end 1999)[1]	5,881
GDP per capita (Purchasing Power Standards)(per cent of EU average)(1999)[1]	28
GDP at current prices (billion euros)(1999)[1]	173
Inflation rate, annual average (January–September 2000**)[1]	60.4
Appreciation/depreciation of national currency against the euro/Ecu (2001) (1997=100)[3]	21.57

Sources: [1] Eurostat (2000); [2] IMF (2000) *World Economic Outlook Database*, September; [3] Datastream.

Notes: * Eurostat defines Purchasing Power Standards as an artificial currency to enable correct comparison of volume of goods and services produced by different countries. Figures have been calculated using the population figures from National Accounts, which may differ from those used in demographic statistics.
** Moving 12-month average rate of change.

PROCESS OF EU ACCESSION

The evolution of the relationship between Turkey and the EU is summarized in Table 15.2.

The EU recognized Turkey's eligibility to become an official applicant in December 1999 at the Helsinki Summit. While this recognition bestowed the right to Turkey ultimately to join the EU when the country is ready, at the same time the EU was concerned with the serious problems and the contradictions of this country. One of the major problems obstructing Turkey's accession is the unresolved issue of the rights of the Kurdish minority.

Table 15.2 Evolution of the relationship between Turkey and the EU

Date	Stage of application	Additional comments
September 1963	Association Agreement (Ankara Agreement) signed between the European Community and Turkey[1]	The Association Agreement foresaw Turkey's full entry into the European Economic Community (EEC)
April 1987	Official application for EU membership submitted[1]	
March 1995	The Turkey–EU Association Council reached a conclusion on the Customs Union[1]	The Customs Union entered into effect on 1 January 1996 and was authorized by the European Parliament
December 1997	Luxembourg Summit[1]	Turkey was not included in the accession process planned by the European Council
June 1998	Cardiff Summit: Turkey's 'European Strategy' endorsed by the EU[1]	The Strategy failed to establish a foundation on which to build Turkey's accession process
October 1998	The Commission issued the first of a series of Regular Reports on Turkey	Aimed at Vienna European Council
June 1999	Cologne Summit[1]	No further headway was made on Turkey's progress to accession
October 1999	The Commission issued the second series of Regular Reports	Aimed at Helsinki European Council; Commission proposed that Turkey be considered as an 'official applicant'
December 1999	The EU declared Turkey an official candidate for full membership in the EU	Approved at the Council Meeting
April 2000	EC–Turkey Association Council meeting in Luxembourg adopted important decisions for the period ahead (i.e. the pre-accession strategy)[2]	Included Accession Partnership and National Programme; eight sub-committees were formed to: ■ carry out a 'screening' of the *acquis*. This was with the objective of enhancing the conformity of Turkey's rules and regulations with that of the community

Date	Stage of application	Additional comments
April 2000 (cont.)		■ ensure the most pressing aspects of the Accession Partnership are put in place
June 2000	EC–Turkey Joint Parliamentary Committee[3]	A 'joint resolution' was agreed on (this had not occurred previously)
July 2000	1 The Commission adopted a single framework for co-ordinating all sources of EU financial assistance for pre-accession. It established the legal base to draw up an Accession Partnership for Turkey and defined a single framework for co-ordinating all sources of EU financial assistance to Turkey for pre-accession[3] 2 EC–Turkey Joint Consultative Committee on economic and social affairs held in Izmir	The most recent changes in the relationship between Turkey and the EU and the decoupling of services and public sector contracts from the Government were debated
November 2000	The Commission issued the third series of Regular Reports	

Sources: [1] Directorate General of Press and Information, Turkey (1999) *Foreign Policy of Turkey*, Reference Series No. 8, July, Ankara; [2] Republic of Turkey, Ministry of Foreign Affairs (2000) *The Latest Situation of Turkey–EU Relations*, April; [3] European Commission (2000) *Regular Report on Turkey's Progress Towards Accession*, November.

While there is some element of interplay of market forces, the Turkish Government still maintains a strong foothold in the economy and protects the country from the forces of the market. The Government's basic industry ventures produce around 8 per cent of GDP (at the start of 2001). These ventures are unprofitable and employ an unnecessary number of workers; hence, they are reliant on governmental financial support. The figure is still too high by EU standards.

The coalition Government is in agreement on most important economic issues, and the Government's dedication to modernize Turkey's economic, social and political standing is evident in a number of policies that have been approved by the Parliament. There is a basic agreement that modernization is a necessity, although some are opposed to the damage caused to society in the short term. This could have been given more consideration in the preliminary stages of reform – the pressures imposed on society will now have to be rectified.

Streamlining is necessary within the Government itself. In particular there is a need for greater harmonization between different ministries.[1]

MEETING EU REQUIREMENTS FOR ENTRY

Turkey does not meet the political or economic Copenhagen Criteria, and pre-accession talks on the *acquis* are still in the preliminary stages. At the EC–Turkey Association Council of April 2000, eight sub-committees were established to monitor and assist Turkey in meeting its obligations under the *acquis*. The following areas have been discussed:

- agriculture
- fisheries
- transport
- energy
- environment
- the internal market.

Although Turkey has compiled a list of the necessary legislation to pass in compliance with the *acquis*, further sub-committee meetings will be necessary – and are indeed planned – for a better assessment of the state of Turkey's compatibility with the EU.

Meeting political criteria

Unfortunately Turkey's political performance still hinders its chances of joining the EU. Accession may not occur for a long time, possibly not before 2010. Relations with the EU may fray, as the Government denies discrimination against the Kurds. As far as the Turkish Government is concerned, the Kurds in Turkey are treated as equals.[2]

The Cyprus problem also remains a concern to the European Commission. Turkey, however, has elsewhere objected to this issue, claiming that it fulfils its obligation to the island – that of 'peace-keeping'. As far as Turkey is concerned, each side of the island is an independent state in its own right.[3]

Meeting economic criteria

The level of government intervention by Turkey still protects the economy from market forces. State firms still operate the basic industry sector. These firms are both inefficient and heavily reliant on governmental financial support.

The Government still controls 25 per cent of prices in the components of the consumer price index (CPI).

There is a need for a greater transparency, efficiency and a more rigorous approach to law enforcement.

Although the level of price inflation had dropped since 1999 to 49 per cent in September 2000 (a level that had not been achieved since the beginning of the 1990s), it is still excessively high.

Meeting obligations of membership

Accession negotiations have not begun as yet and consequently no chapters of the *acquis* have been opened.

TIMING OF ACCESSION

In some EU circles, there is a view that Turkey is an applicant country that could be permanently in the waiting room. At the other extreme, there are those very few who maintain that Turkey's journey towards EU membership should be relatively swift. This, they argue, is due to the fact that Turkey has become acquainted with the majority of laws and policies applied in the EU, with whom the country has had a long-standing relationship since 1963. The results of this study suggest this view is not valid.

As has been shown in the scenarios outlined in Chapter 2, Turkey can be placed in a category of its own. Certain developments could speed up the country's accession process. However, many sensitive issues, including disagreements with the EU itself, threaten to prolong the process.

Turkey has yet to achieve macroeconomic stability. The financial crisis of early December 2000 is a potent example of the volatile nature of the Turkish economy. Two perspectives can be taken on this development:

(i) The financial crisis fuels the argument that Turkey will indefinitely remain in the waiting room.

(ii) The financial crisis is a blessing in disguise. Turkey will now be more closely monitored and scrutinized by Europe and the rest of the world. With the IMF providing financial support, the Government is compelled to instigate economic reform. The Government has set itself rather ambitious objectives, including reducing inflation to 12 per cent in 2001 (and to single figures in 2002[4]) from 39 per cent at the end of 2000. On the external trade side, the Government intends to hold the current account deficit below 3.5 per cent of GNP in 2001 and under 3 per cent in 2002.[5] Further priorities are to:

- speed up the reduction of public debt through a more rigorous fiscal policy;

- fortify the banking sector;

- promote privatization.[6]

A concerted effort towards reform may accelerate Turkey's progress in fulfilling both the economic and political Copenhagen Criteria.

In light of the above obstacles to EU entry, it is evident that Turkey's accession prospects are far from clear cut. Numerous problems need to be corrected and resolved. It is possible that economic reforms will enhance the accession process, although the colossal magnitude of work to be done (both from the economic and political viewpoints) prevents any entry by the country before 2010.

Notes

1   European Commission (2000) *Regular Report on Turkey's Progress Towards Accession*, November.

2   Turkish Ministry of Foreign Affairs (2000) *Press Release No. 217 in response to the Morillon Report Regarding Turkey's Progress Towards Accession*, 15 November.

3   Ibid.

4   Turkish Government (2000) *Turkey Letter of Intent*, 18 December. (This letter was presented by the Turkish Government to Horst Kohler, Managing Director IMF.)

5   Ibid.

6   Ibid.

Part three

16

Reform of EU institutions

THE FUTURE STRUCTURE OF THE EU

On 7 December 2000 the European Council[1] met at Nice for a summit to formulate a new treaty that would reform the EU institutions. The main focus of this Council meeting was to restructure the *modus operandi* of the EU institutions to allow the smooth functioning of an enlarged Union with almost double the size of its existing member states (up to 28 member states). An expanded EU with 28 members is within sight when all the existing 13 official applicant countries are admitted. However, the EU could become a great deal larger, with possibly ten other countries in the pipeline.

The European institutions, which were originally designed for a mere six member states (based on the Treaty of Rome), would have to manage in future a Union of nearly five times (if not seven times) that size. To amend the Treaty and prepare the EU for the accession of new member states, it was necessary to assemble a new Intergovernmental Conference (IGC) with representatives of the governments of the member states. The IGC and the subsequent Nice Summit were designed to revise the founding Treaty of Rome, which was originally signed as long ago as 1957.

RESHAPING OF THE EXISTING EU ARRANGEMENTS

An intergovernmental conference (IGC) which has been a long-running conference of the 15 member states was called for the reform of EU institutions and began its round of meetings on 14 February 2000. It concluded its mandate with the Nice European Council on 11 December 2000. This IGC was first established at the European Council of Cologne, when Germany had its presidency of the Union (January–June 1999) and was further reinforced at Helsinki (December 1999). The mission of this IGC was to examine:

- the size and the composition of the Commission;

- the weighting of votes in the Council;

- the extension of the votes of qualified majority to other areas;

- some other institutional issues, such as the enhanced power of the President.

In June 2000, during the presidency of Portugal, the Council of Feira prepared a progress report on the reform of EU institutions and it formally included the topic of 'enhanced co-operation' (further explained below). The European Council in Biarritz (on 13–14 October 2000) prepared the foundation for an agreement in Nice. At the same time, a meeting of representatives of the European institutions and the national parliaments prepared a Charter of Fundamental Rights, which has been subsequently approved by the heads of states and government. The Charter was approved at the European Council at Nice.

PRINCIPAL AREAS OF REFORM AGREED IN NICE

The main aim of the reforms is to change the EU institutions and the decision-making rules to make the Union as a bloc more effective when new countries join. The EU has so far opened negotiations with 12 countries and is also undergoing pre-accession discussions with Turkey.

Voting power for each country

Nearly two-thirds of the European Council's decisions are taken by means of a voting system known as qualified majority voting (QMV). Under the pre-Nice regime (which will continue until 2005), for a qualified majority to win, there have to be 62 votes out of the total of 87. Thus a mixture of over 25 votes could block any decision. For instance, the combined voting strength of the Southern European countries (Italy, Spain, Portugal and Greece) adds up to a total of 28 votes, and this voting power can be used to suit the countries concerned.[2]

An example of where QMV was used to make an important European decision is the case of European Monetary Union (EMU). In May 1998 the European Council applied qualified majority voting[3] as the basis of its decision to select the countries participating in EMU. For this purpose all the 15 member states of the European Council voted, even though at that time four member states did not join the single currency.

Prior to the Nice Agreement only 20 per cent of the EU decisions required unanimous approval by all the member states. This implies that even if one member state (out of the existing 15 members) objects, the decision would not go through and the policy would not be implemented. This 'right to object' is known as the 'right of veto' and guarantees that the national interests of the member state in question are observed. It also guarantees that all member countries participate (and are in agreement) in matters related to important decisions, including issues such as taxation.

The original aim of the Nice Summit was to extend the QMV system to around 50 subject matters. The main problem was to choose which areas could be managed by QMV and which areas need the support of every member state. The Treaty of Nice has extended the QMV system to 29 areas,[4] including international trade and industrial policy.

Suffice it to say, the voting rights could play an important part in the final shape of the EU and will form the ultimate tactical bargaining position for countries.

The Pre-Nice Qualified Majority Voting

It was considered by the EU members that the existing system of QMV does not adequately reflect the countries' populations – hence, making the system somewhat undemocratic. The existing system is depicted in Table 16.1, with Germany, Italy,

France and the UK each having ten votes, Spain eight and the others fewer, falling to two for Luxembourg. This structure was too biased in favour of the smaller countries, who enjoyed a proportionally greater weight relative to the size of their population. Therefore, a reform was introduced at the Nice Summit.

Table 16.1 The existing (pre-Nice) weight (qualified majority voting) of the 15 member states of the EU (until 1 January 2005)

Member state	Population (million)	Number of votes	Current weight (%)	Number of European Commissioners	Seats in Parliament
Germany	82.038	10	11.49	2	99
UK	59.247	10	11.49	2	87
France	58.966	10	11.49	2	87
Italy	57.610	10	11.49	2	87
Spain	39.394	8	9.20	2	64
Netherlands	15.760	5	5.75	1	31
Greece	10.533	5	5.75	1	25
Belgium	10.213	5	5.75	1	25
Portugal	9.980	5	5.75	1	25
Sweden	8.854	4	4.60	1	22
Austria	8.082	4	4.60	1	21
Denmark	5.313	3	3.45	1	16
Finland	5.160	3	3.45	1	16
Ireland	3.744	3	3.45	1	15
Luxembourg	0.429	2	2.30	1	6
Total	375.323	87	100	20	626

Sources: Eurostat (2000); European Parliament (2000).

Reweighting of Qualified Majority Voting

Table 16.2 presents the voting rights of EU member states after the Nice Treaty. It depicts how both the Qualified Majority Voting (QMV) system and the Parliamentary system have been reformed.[5] As a result of the reforms, countries with larger populations are assigned slightly more votes. For example, the share of each of the large countries has increased from 11.49 per cent of the total votes (87) to 12.24 per cent of the total votes (becoming 237 votes before any new country joins). However, a bloc vote among the bigger countries could only muster 49 per cent of the total, whereas prior to the reform their share was 46 per cent of the total number of votes.

Table 16.2 Voting rights of EU member states after the Nice Treaty

Member state	Population (million)	Weighted votes pre-Nice	Weighted votes pre-Nice (% of total)	Reformed weighted votes from 2005	Reformed weighted votes from 2005 (% of total)	Parliamentary allocation of seats	
						Old	New
Germany	82.038	10	11.49	29	12.24	99	99
UK	59.247	10	11.49	29	12.24	87	72
France	58.966	10	11.49	29	12.24	87	72
Italy	57.610	10	11.49	29	12.24	87	72
Spain	39.394	8	9.20	27	11.39	64	50
Netherlands	15.760	5	5.75	13	5.49	31	25
Greece	10.533	5	5.75	12	5.06	25	20
Belgium	10.213	5	5.75	12	5.06	25	22
Portugal	9.980	5	5.75	12	5.06	25	20
Sweden	8.854	4	4.60	10	4.22	22	18
Austria	8.082	4	4.60	10	4.22	21	17
Denmark	5.313	3	3.45	7	2.95	16	13
Finland	5.160	3	3.45	7	2.95	16	13
Ireland	3.744	3	3.45	7	2.95	15	12
Luxembourg	0.429	2	2.30	4	1.69	6	6
Total	375.323	87	100	237	100	626	531

Source: European Council (2000) Treaty of Nice.

The agreement reached at the Nice Summit allocated the same weighting for Germany (29) as that of France, Italy and the UK in terms of the qualified votes in the Council. All the large countries will have 29 votes, while Spain has 27, Netherlands 13, Belgium, Greece and Portugal 12, Sweden and Austria 10, Denmark, Finland and Ireland 7, and Luxembourg 4.

In the new reformed system, with 12 applicant countries admitted (*see* Table 16.3), there will be a total of 345 votes.[6] Accordingly QMV would be reached under the following conditions:

Acts of the Council shall require for their adoption at least 258 votes in favour, cast by a majority of members, where this Treaty requires them to be adopted on a proposal from the Commission.

In other cases, for their adoption acts of the Council shall require at least 258 votes in favour cast by at least two-thirds of the members.

When a decision is to be adopted by the Council by a qualified majority, a member of the Council may request verification that the Member States constituting the qualified majority represent at least 62% of the total population of the Union. If that condition is shown not to have been met, the decision in question shall not be adopted.

Table 16.3 Voting rights of EU members in an enlarged EU – a comparison with the pre-Nice structure

Member state	Population (million)	Weighted votes pre-Nice*	Weighted votes pre-Nice (% of total)	Weighted votes agreed at Nice	Weighted votes agreed at Nice (% of total)
Germany	82.038	10	7.75	29	8.41
UK	59.247	10	7.75	29	8.41
France	58.966	10	7.75	29	8.41
Italy	57.610	10	7.75	29	8.41
Spain	39.394	8	6.20	27	7.83
Netherlands	15.760	5	3.88	13	3.77
Greece	10.533	5	3.88	12	3.48
Belgium	10.213	5	3.88	12	3.48
Portugal	9.980	5	3.88	12	3.48
Sweden	8.854	4	3.10	10	2.90
Austria	8.082	4	3.10	10	2.90
Denmark	5.313	3	2.33	7	2.03
Finland	5.160	3	2.33	7	2.03
Ireland	3.744	3	2.33	7	2.03
Luxembourg	0.429	2	1.55	4	1.16
Poland	38.667	(8)	6.20	27	7.83
Romania	22.489	(5)	3.88	14	4.06

Member state	Population (million)	Weighted votes pre-Nice*	Weighted votes pre-Nice (% of total)	Weighted votes agreed at Nice	Weighted votes agreed at Nice (% of total)
Czech Republic	10.290	(5)	3.88	12	3.48
Hungary	10.092	(5)	3.88	12	3.48
Bulgaria	8.230	(4)	3.10	10	2.90
Slovakia	5.393	(3)	2.33	7	2.03
Lithuania	3.701	(3)	2.33	7	2.03
Latvia	2.439	(2)	1.55	4	1.16
Slovenia	1.978	(2)	1.55	4	1.16
Estonia	1.446	(2)	1.55	4	1.16
Cyprus	0.752	(2)	1.55	4	1.16
Malta	0.379	(1)	0.78	3	0.87
Total	481.179	(129)	100	345	100

Source: European Commission (2000) *Treaty of Nice*.

* Votes indicated in brackets are estimated on the basis of the pre-Nice summit structure and are estimated in consultation with the European Commission.

The combined population of the largest four countries is 257 million, comprising 54 per cent of the total population of the enlarged EU. Nevertheless, the largest four countries together possess only a total of 116 votes – a number that is far from the required 258 votes. Therefore, they would not be able to dominate the decision-making process.

The reformed voting rights could play an important part in the final shape of the EU decision-making process and will form the ultimate tactical bargaining position for countries. Under the new regime, reaching a qualified majority could still prove difficult.

When the Nice Treaty comes into effect

Article 3 of the Treaty of Nice states:

Provisions concerning the weighting of votes in the Council
1. On 1 January 2005:
(i) Article 205(2) and (4) of the Treaty establishing the European Community shall be amended as follows:
2. Where the Council is required to act by a qualified majority, the votes of its members shall be weighted as follows:

Belgium   *12*
Denmark   *7*

Germany	29
Greece	12
Spain	27
France	29
Ireland	7
Italy	29
Luxembourg	4
Netherlands	13
Austria	10
Portugal	12
Finland	7
Sweden	10
United Kingdom	29

Acts of the Council shall require for their adoption at least 169 votes in favour cast by at least a majority of the members where this Treaty requires them to be adopted on a proposal from the Commission. In other cases, for their adoption acts of the Council shall require at least 169 votes in favour, cast by at least two-thirds of the members.

...

4. When a decision is to be adopted by the Council by a qualified majority, a member of the Council may request verification that the qualified majority comprises at least 62% of the total population of the Union. If that condition is shown not to have been met, the decision in question shall not be adopted.".(ii) Corresponding amendments shall be made to the third subparagraph of Article 23(2) and to Article 34(3) of the Treaty on European Union.

2. At the time of each accession, the threshold referred to in the second subparagraph of Article 205(2) of the Treaty establishing the European Community shall be calculated in such a way that the qualified majority threshold expressed in votes does not exceed the threshold resulting from the table in the Declaration to be included in the Final Act of the Conference on the enlargement of the EU.

THE FUTURE FORMAT OF THE EUROPEAN COMMISSION

The Nice Summit decided that, starting from 2005, Germany, France, the UK, Italy and Spain would lose their second commissioners. The candidate countries will each have one commissioner.

The original French proposal was to keep the number of commissioners down to the existing 20. It had proposed to rotate the commissioners among countries rather than boost their number to 27 or 28, even after the EU admits 12 or 13 new members. If the member countries of the EU were more than 20, equal rotation would have been given starting from 2010.

France argued that maintaining one commissioner per country could lead to a Commission with some 27–28 executives to embrace all the member countries. This could run the risk of being unmanageable.

Prior to the Nice Agreement some countries, such as Italy,[7] were not willing to adhere to the principle of at least one commissioner for each member state. They wished to keep two commissioners for the larger countries. This proposal was not in the end accepted by the countries, and the final decision was for one commissioner per country.

The Nice Summit and the resulting Treaty further strengthened the power of the President of the Commission. He/she will be able to allocate and to redistribute the assignments of the commissioners. The President will also be able to name the Vice-President and to manage the organization of the Commission.

UNANIMITY – THE RIGHT OF VETO

The Nice Summit discussed the removal of the veto, to enable some countries to work on projects with closer collaboration. This would allow some members to move ahead with integration faster than others, creating the prospect of a 'Europe with two speeds'.

The struggle for power

The crucial issue on which there was the strongest resistance at the Nice Summit on the part of several countries was related to the extension of qualified majority voting:

■ the UK[8] did not wish to renounce the right of veto on the state treasury;

■ Spain, one of the biggest beneficiaries of regional aid, blocked the abolition of the unanimity on EU funds;

■ the Nordic countries wanted to keep the veto on emergency and social protection;

■ Italy[9] and Germany were determined to reduce to the minimum the areas in which the right of veto is maintained.

Regarding a new balance of voting power, one of the main problems of EU institutional reform was between France and Germany. Prior to the Nice Summit, Chancellor Schröder had insisted on Germany having more votes than those of Italy, France and the UK, on the grounds that Germany's population was greater (by 20 million) than each of the three other countries. On the other hand, France's President Chirac was against every solution that could give more power to Germany.

STEPS TOWARD FURTHER EUROPEAN INTEGRATION

One of the main obstacles to a faster integration is the right of a member country to veto the combined decision of the other member states.

Enhanced co-operation

The issue on which European countries made greater progress was in the area of enhanced co-operation. Almost all the countries were in favour. A closer collaboration would allow some countries to develop faster in some fields and it could be more suitable for a future larger EU with economic and geographical differentiation. The main objection to this process came from the UK and the Nordic countries, who are against an enhanced co-operation in defence matters.

The final agreement of the Nice Summit allows eight or more members to move forward with faster integration in specific areas. This, however, excludes enhanced co-operation in matters related to defence.

The Charter of Fundamental Rights

The Nice Summit also considered social questions by passing an EU Charter of Fundamental Rights. The text, approved in October 2000 in Biarritz, was divided into six topics: dignity, fundamental freedom, equality, solidarity, civil rights and justice. There were two options:

- there was the idea of a constitution that defines the concept of European citizenship and extends individual rights within the EU;
- the other possibility was more political and looked at a constitution that simplifies the organization of the European entity.

At the Nice Summit the possibility of incorporating this Charter in the Treaty was also discussed, thus creating a first basis for a European Constitution.

Finally, there was a great deal of concern about the possibility of incorporating in the Treaty the Charter of Fundamental Rights. Some countries argued that it is time for Europe to have its own proper Constitution. The UK did not support this idea. For those against a European Constitution this was considered as an infringement of national sovereignty.

THE RESPONSE OF SOME MEMBER STATES

The Italian position was moderately positive. Following the Nice Summit on 13 December 2000 the Italian Prime Minister, Giuliano Amato, reported to the Italian Committee for Foreign Affairs on the outcome of the Summit. The most rewarding outcome was that the 15 member states had managed to reach an agreement. A failure would have had serious consequences for Europe and its enlargement.

Some doubts still remained as to the effectiveness of the new voting system. The dilution of the voting rights and further strengthening of the big countries was regarded by the Italians as not necessarily that helpful for the EU decision-making process. In this system it is quite easy to form a blocking minority coalition.

The agreement on enhanced co-operation and increasing of the power of the President of the Commission were considered by the Italians as one of the best results of this Summit. Consequently, some eight or more countries can move ahead with faster integration without being blocked by the veto of the other member states.

EU REFORM AND THE EURO

The impact of the Summit on the financial market was at first fairly neutral. Subsequently, however, in December 2000–January 2001 the euro began to strengthen against the US dollar, gradually reaching some $0.95. Most of the reason for the euro's strengthening was due to the weakening of the US economy and, hence, the dollar. Nevertheless, one of the main reasons for the weakness of the euro has been the uncertainty surrounding the sustainability of the European integration. A failure of the meeting would have been negative for the euro because it would have highlighted the weak unity of the member countries at a time when the financial markets had hoped to witness a greater unity, at least towards European Monetary Union.

Notes

1   Meeting of heads of member states/governments of the EU.

2   In practice, however, the decisions of the European Council tend to be unanimous.

3   The Maastricht Treaty required that 'the Council, acting by a qualified majority on a recommendation from the Commission, shall assess: for each Member State, whether it fulfils the necessary conditions for the adoption of a single currency'. *The 'Official Journal' of the European Communities* (1992) C224, (35), p. 42.

4   European Council (2000) *Treaty of Nice: Provisional text approved by the Intergovernmental Conference on Institutional Reforms.*

5   Ibid, pp. 74–79.

6   Ibid, p. 79.

7   Ministero degli Affari Esteri (2000) *La Conferenza Intergovernativa sulla Revisione dei Trattati: la posizione dell'Italia.*

8   Discussions with Foreign and Commonwealth Office (2000).

9   Ministero degli Affari Esteri (2000) *La Conferenza Intergovernativa sulla Revisione dei Trattati: la posizione dell'Italia.*